Men Against the Sea

Men Against the Sea

by Ross R. Olney

PUBLISHERS   Grosset & Dunlap   NEW YORK

To Jim Auxier and Chuck Blakeslee
and our adventures on ships, submarines and submersibles
and to Jon Hardy
who taught me to dive

Acknowledgment

The author wishes to thank the following for photos, advice and technical information:

CHAN BUSH, *Photographer* • BOB JOHNSON, *Photographer* • The National Archives • Wide World Photos • The National Geographic Society • The *Cleveland Plain Dealer* • BOB DUNN, *Photographer* • U.S. Naval Photographic Center • Gerald G. Kallman Associates • A. M. ADAMS, *London Daily Mirror* • ROBERT HOWARD, Global Marine • U.S. Navy Electronics Laboratory • Westinghouse Electric Corporation • JONATHAN DODD, Dodd, Mead & Company, Inc. • RON W. COOK, North American Rockwell Corp. • BEULAH HAGEN, Harper & Row, *Publishers* • Ocean Systems Division, North American Aviation • J. C. SHIELDS, Naval Undersea Warfare Center • GEORGE A. JOHNSON, J. Walter Thompson Co. • WALTER H. SCOTT, JR., Grumman Aircraft Engineering Corp. • ROBERT A. WEBB, Lt. Col., USAF, Office of the Asst. Sec. of Defense. And especially CONNIE JOHNSON, Managing Editor of *Skin Diver Magazine,* for her enthusiastic and generous support, and for several years of fine friendship.

Contents

Introduction · 1

Hannes Keller · 5

Simon Lake · 19

Jacques-Yves Cousteau · 29

Thor Heyerdahl · 41

Auguste and Jacques Piccard · 53

Robert N. Manry · 65

Andreas B. Rechnitzer · 77

Francis Chichester · 89

John Ridgway and Chay Blyth · 99

Charles B. "Swede" Momsen · 107

William Willis · 117

Edward Ellsberg · 125

Robert F. Dill · 135

Introduction

There are many ways to combat the vast oceans of the world. Some men try to win over the sea by taking from her the secrets she holds. They attempt to dive deep and survive the crushing pressure and the strange diving diseases. When they return, if they return, they bring some of the secrets of the sea with them. Others attempt to sail, or row, or drift across the face of the sea in flimsy vessels, challenging the sea to try to stop them.

Some men challenge the sea on a scientific level. With their chemicals and test tubes they attempt to wrest precious materials from her. Others try to put the great forces in her currents and tides to work for man. Still others probe at the life within her, attempting to learn the secrets of these life forms for the good of man.

Men punch and drill at the sea bottom to locate the vast natural resources known to be there. Always the sea waits for a mistake and then, usually, man must pay for his search for knowledge, or adventure, or supremacy, for the sea is an unforgiving adversary.

She can quickly and without a sign of mercy take the life of a man who has approached her without knowledge and planning and respect. Yet approach her we must, for the sea has always been of great importance to man, and she becomes increasingly important as man comes to realize that his very life may soon depend upon her.

For the number of people on earth is increasing day by day. Each day, as this population continues to expand, fewer natural resources are available.

The one grows . . . the other lessens. At least, on dry land. But the sea, that vast untapped area of food and water and chemicals and metals, stands ready to provide man with more resources than he has used in his entire history on earth, and more than he could use for thousands of years yet.

In only one cubic mile of ocean water (and there are three hundred million such cubic miles in all) there are about 160,000,000 tons of valuable solids waiting to serve man, if he can learn to extract them. These solids are worth about $6,000,000,000 to man today. Not including fish and marine organisms, they still represent only one three hundred millionth of the wealth available. Including fish, these solids represent food for the world for as far ahead as man cares to look. One chemist determined that each single cubic meter of sea water contains 1.5 grams of protein and 3.9 grams of carbo-hydrates in plankton growth. This equals the nutritive value of twenty thousand world grain harvests in the Atlantic Ocean alone.

Yes, the sea has always been, and will always be, of incalculable impor-tance to man, and though she is totally unforgiving, he will continue to attempt to wrest from her the secrets and the supremacy she holds. The men in this book are some of the best known, and most courageous, of these ocean fighters.

Men Against the Sea

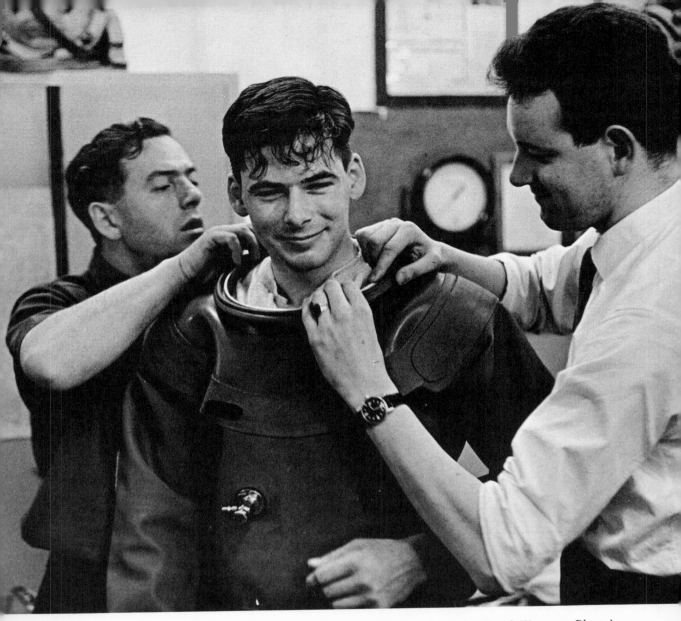

Hannes Keller prepares to enter the wet diving tank at the Naval Weapons Plant in Washington, D. C. for a simulated dive to 700 feet. Every condition which might be met in the sea is faced in this controlled dive with the exception of cold or marine life.

(U.S. NAVY PHOTO)

Hannes Keller

THE MISTY, gray dawn of December 3, 1962, rose over an odd assembly of ships off the coast of Southern California, near Catalina Island. Among them were the usual number of small craft that always cluster nearby when anything exciting is happening on the water. Also present was the observer boat *Whirlaway,* whose passenger list that morning included reporters and photographers from the world's leading newspapers, wire services, and magazines.

The center of all this attention was an ungainly barge, the *Eureka,* owned by the Shell Oil Company. On its deck, attached to a crane by a thin steel cable, was the cause of all the curiosity—the diving bell *Atlantis.*

None of the onlookers had trouble seeing it—even at a distance—for it had been painted a bright yellow for easy visibility far down in the ocean depths. Standing upon a base rack that held over a dozen high-pressure gas bottles, the bell itself seemed just large enough for two grown men to stoop inside. American and Swiss flags were painted on the outside, and each bottle on the rack beneath it was prominently numbered. Tubes passed from the bottles through a mixing device inside the bell. Floodlights which bathed the yellow submersible gave the scene an eerie quality.

The deck of the *Eureka*—a drilling platform—bustled with activity. Last-minute details were checked and rechecked, including the functioning of closed-circuit television cameras mounted inside and outside the bell. The pictures transmitted to a monitor in the cabin of the *Eureka* would be the only visual proof of the success—or failure—of the coming experiment.

5

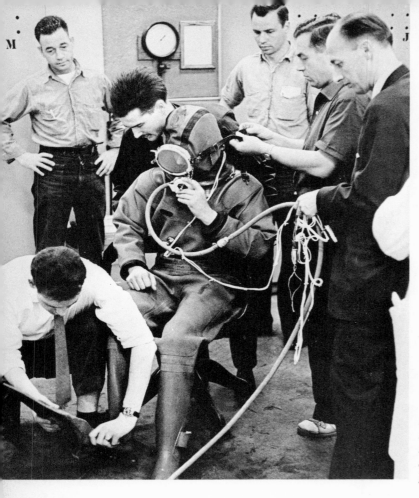

Keller's ascent time was much shorter than normally required by standard diving tables, due to his own secret mixture of breathing gases. (U.S. NAVY PHOTO)

One man was particularly busy, for his work of a lifetime was about to be tested. His own life was also at stake.

The sea can be a cruel enemy and snuff out human life in many ways. On its surface, a man can be battered, beaten and finally driven under to drown. Deep under its surface, the sea can be even more cruel. Tons of pressure, squeezing at the body of a man, force gases into his blood that can cause agonizing pain and can also kill. Here he can suffer the dreaded "rapture of the deep," nitrogen narcosis, and become like someone lost in a pleasant dream. He may even discard his air supply, sure in his own addled mind that the sea will not harm him.

Or, worse, he may suffer the "bends," the insidious diving disease that allows a man to dive deep into the ocean, but then will not allow him to rise

6

again without excruciating pain and eventual death. At a depth of only thirty-three feet, nitrogen gas is driven into the bloodstream by the enormous pressure of the ocean. Then, if the diver attempts to rise too soon, or too fast, this gas can bubble into his blood and joints, just as the gases inside a carbonated drink will bubble when the cap is removed and pressure is loosened. First pain will come, and death will follow unless the man is promptly recompressed in a pressure tank and then decompressed more slowly.

The busy man on the deck of the *Eureka* had spent years developing a formula of gases that would rob the ocean of its power to cause the bends. His name—Hannes Keller—was already known in international diving circles, for this intrepid young Swiss scientist, professor and mathematician was trying to prove something that thus far had been deemed impossible.

Keller returns to the "surface" in the pressure tank during his dive to 700 feet. He is unaffected by his short decompression time. (U.S. NAVY PHOTO)

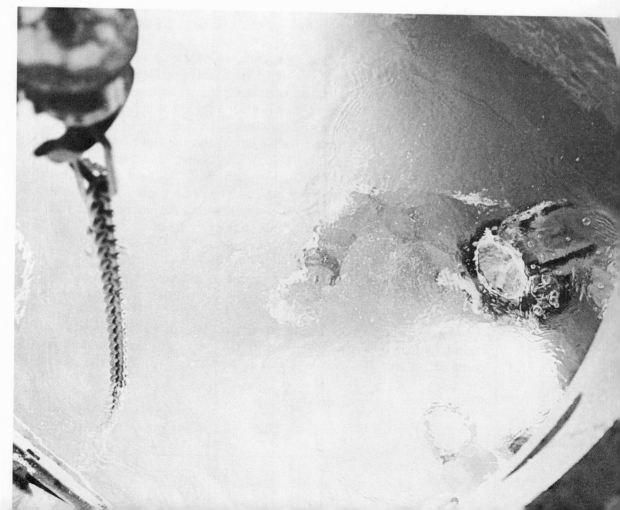

Fear of the bends had not prevented men from risking the dreadful penalties that might result from deep diving. Divers had always been able to penetrate to great depths if proper decompressing methods followed. But decompression from a deep dive would often require hours, or even days, to complete. Either the diver had to be brought very slowly to the surface, or brought up rapidly and then promptly lodged in a pressure chamber for the tedious decompression process. In no case could a diver go much below four or five hundred feet, even on experimental dives, since decompression would take far too long to make the effort worthwhile. A diver working at greater depths could not really accomplish much during the short time he was able to stay below. And afterward he had to spend days recovering from the ordeal in a recompression chamber.

This was the way it had been until Hannes Keller found a weapon with which to combat this age-old menace to divers. By applying his formula of gases, he was convinced, man could descend one thousand feet—perhaps even deeper—and still return to the surface in a relatively brief period without fear of bends or nitrogen narcosis. He had worked long and hard, and had already risked his life to confirm his theory, and now he stood at the threshold of first proof.

Keller was confident that this real test would be a success. No thought of possible failure—or tragedy—entered his mind. For Hannes Keller, aided by his precise, scientific habits, had prepared himself thoroughly for this moment. Years of painstaking research had preceded the great experiment about to be conducted in the deep waters off Catalina.

The dive that convinced Keller he was on the right track took place in 1959 in the Lake of Zurich in Switzerland. Keller was then twenty-six years old with only two years of diving experience behind him. His equipment was rudimentary and homemade. An old gasoline drum had been transformed into a diving bell at a total cost of one dollar—four large compressed-air tanks were strapped around the drum, and the inner tube of an automobile tire was taken along in case of an emergency ascent.

With this primitive diving gear, and his own theories, Keller reached a depth of four hundred feet, and returned to the surface much more quickly than the current dive tables allowed. And he had not, as divers say, become "bent."

So his sharp, inquiring mind carried his theory a step further. Why couldn't a man dive much deeper, with the proper gas mixtures, and return in complete safety? His own first dive had apparently proved the old theories wrong. Turning to Dr. Albert Buhlmann, of the cardio-pulmonary section of Zurich University, Keller began to search for answers. Buhlmann became interested in the young professor's ideas, and the two men decided that deep diving could be accomplished with much shorter decompression if the diver breathed a controlled mixture of different gases that would prevent nitrogen bubbles from invading the bloodstream.

The IBM World Trade Corporation, always interested in new scientific advances, provided a data-processing machine that could compute Keller's mathematical formulations. In a remarkably short time, the IBM 650 had calculated and checked more than 250,000 four-figure numbers as it compiled

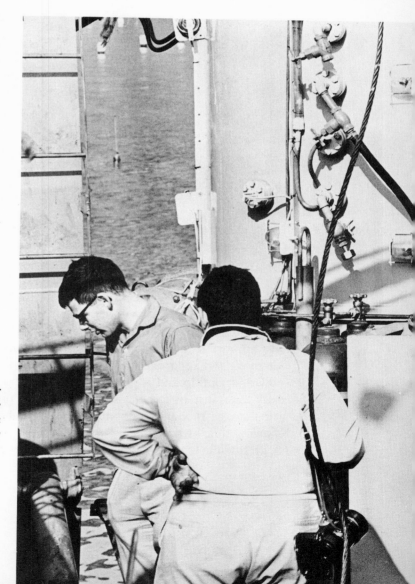

On the deck of the Eureka, Keller *checks last moment details before his dive to 1000 feet off Catalina in the final test of his breathing gases.* (BOB JOHNSON PHOTO)

Dick Anderson (left) and Chris Whittaker (right) chat with magazine editor Connie Johnson before suiting-up to serve as safety divers on Keller's record-breaking dive. Whittaker died during the experiment. (BOB JOHNSON PHOTO)

four hundred new decompression tables for depths of 1,312 feet and under. The job would have taken Keller—or any other human mathematician—more than two years to complete.

All that remained was the practical proof, and for this a man would have to actually dive into the crushing depths. Since the entire idea had been Keller's, he volunteered to undergo the test.

Hannes Keller, a brilliant scientist, is also a man of action. His personality appears to be made up of contradictions that nevertheless live together side by side in apparent harmony. He is, at one and the same time, daring and shrewd, scientific and a gambler. Careful and calculating in his work, he is ready in an instant to bet his own life on an unproven theory. Handsome and articulate, he is equally at home among his fellow professors or in diving gear. Knowing this, one is not surprised that Keller—as he did constantly—laid his life on the line to demonstrate his scientific beliefs.

In August, 1960, Keller and Buhlmann arrived at Lake Maggiore in Switzerland. Using the diving tables just computed, and his own mixture of gases, Keller plunged to a world-record depth of 510 feet in four minutes. Then, to the astonishment of observers, he returned to the surface in only thirty minutes, shattering the long-held belief that extensive decompression was essential after deep dives. All accepted decompression tables up to that time stated that a dive to that depth required a five to seven-hour ascent for decompression. A thirty-minute ascent should have killed Keller, yet he suffered no ill effects at all.

Immediately, others became interested in Keller's ideas, and on November 4, 1960, under the supervision of the French Navy, Keller submerged to a simulated depth of 820 feet in ten minutes in the pressure chamber at the Toulon Naval Base. He was brought back to the "surface" (the entire experiment was conducted in a wet pressure chamber) in only forty-nine minutes. Normally, such a deep dive would have required at least eight hours of decompression. An interested and enthusiastic observer of this dive was the famed French underwater expert, Jacques-Yves Cousteau.

Keller's experiments demonstrated that it was possible to make deep descents and to work in areas once believed exceedingly hazardous. This opened up exceptional new opportunities for research and salvage operations. Many wrecks of ships could not be salvaged previously because they were too far down in the ocean. Now—if Keller's methods held up—the out-of-reach and the unattainable were suddenly within the grasp of man. Keller himself mentioned two sunken vessels that might now be salvaged—the giant Italian liner *Andrea Doria* and a German U-Boat, the *U-853,* which had gone down off Block Island in the Atlantic. Both lay below the two hundred-foot level, where no extensive work or salvage could be performed on their hulks.

Until now, Keller's experiments had been conducted in pressure tanks under simulated deep-sea conditions. But would they work in the sea itself? As the experiments continued, Keller knew that the time was approaching when he would have to take his theories out of the laboratory and test them in the real arena where divers had to live and work—the dangerous ocean depths.

And so, early in 1962, Keller began scouting the world for a dive site that would meet his requirements. He eventually chose Catalina Island—off Southern California—"the jewel in the crown of diving." There he found the depth he needed close enough to shore for the support facilities of machine shops, emergency equipment, food and lodging for his crew. He arranged for

The Eureka *oil-drilling platform with its winch over the side. One thousand feet down, suspended from the cable, is the bell of Keller and Small.* (BOB JOHNSON PHOTO)

12

the help of Shell Oil and the United States Navy, both of whom were extremely interested in his deep-ocean research.

It was there, at Catalina, that I met Hannes Keller for the first time. So impressed was I with the young Swiss and his ideas that I even toyed with the notion of accompanying him on his projected dive. Keller wanted someone else to go along with him so he could prove to the experts that his gases would help other divers, too. Rumors had sprung up that Keller was somehow different physically from most human beings, and that his vaunted gas mixtures would only work for him. This, it was said, was the real reason for his phenomenal diving success. These claims, of course, were pure nonsense but Keller was concerned enough to submit to thorough medical examinations so that doctors would confirm he was just an ordinary human and not a superman. My decision not to join Keller on his dive was not due to skepticism. I simply lacked his courage and also his great conviction that he would succeed.

The dive site was finally selected—one mile off Avalon Harbor. Equipment and pressure bottles arrived from Switzerland and a crew was assembled. A confident Hannes Keller arranged all the details and coordinated the preparations for the forthcoming experiment.

By December 3, 1962, everything was ready aboard the *Eureka*. As noon approached, final checks were made. Keller donned his non-pressurized exposure suit, along with another young man, Peter Small, one of Keller's friends who had volunteered to be the other passenger in the diving bell. A journalist by profession, Small, a thirty-five-year-old Englishman, was thus displaying his confidence in Keller by placing his life and his fate squarely in his friend's hands.

On deck also were two other divers who wore standard wet suits and diving tanks. One was Dick Anderson; the other was Christopher Duncan Whittaker, a student at U.C.L.A. Both young men, expert divers, were to act as safety men, though their maximum diving depth was set at two hundred feet.

Keller's plan was to descend one thousand feet, all the way to the bottom, and there to plant a Swiss flag and an American flag on the continental shelf.

The diving bell *Atlantis* was in reality only a safety device, offering no protection from pressures at all. Its bottom was open to the sea. As the bell descended, pressure from the outside water would be equalized inside the bell to keep the water from entering, just as an overturned glass, when held underwater, will still have an air space of tightly compressed air. Thus, both men in the bell would be exposed to the outside pressure, but still would be dry and relatively comfortable. When he reached the bottom, Keller planned to swim down through the hatch and out of the bell, plant the flags, re-enter the bell and seal the bottom hatch.

The seal would contain the pressure while the bell with Keller and Small was lifted to the surface. Once on the surface, the decompression according to Keller's tables could begin. Meanwhile, both men would be protected from marine life and would be exposed only briefly to the intense cold of the depths.

If this experiment worked, Keller planned to make his next dive in a heated suit by swimming to the bottom. Experienced divers and doctors, however, knew that the bell would prove or disprove the young scientist's ideas on gases. Pressure was the real enemy, not the cold or the dangerous marine life.

The two men entered the bell, which was hoisted up and over the side, then lowered. It disappeared in a swirl of water, and the experiment was on. Intent observers watched the television monitors on the barge. Anderson and Whittaker stood by alertly.

Down went the *Atlantis,* deeper and deeper into the black water of the deep ocean, where little light ever penetrates. Huge high-voltage lamps on the bell lighted the water beneath as both men watched for the bottom. Water rose in the open trunk beneath their feet, but was held back at the proper point by the pressure inside. Both men studied the gauges carefully. Everything seemed to be going well. On the surface, men waited tensely, for what Keller and Small were attempting had never been done before, nor had it even been thought possible. Either Keller's secret gas mixtures would protect the two men or they would surely die.

And when they returned to the surface, the pressures inside the bell would have to be released according to Keller's decompression tables instead of those used by other divers. If—and it was a big *if*—Keller and Small did not then suffer the bends, the experiment would have succeeded. If they did, death would come after an interval of excruciating agony.

Down went the bell, ever deeper. The crane on the *Eureka* reeled the holding cable out slowly. Finally, the *Atlantis* settled on the bottom. Viewers watching the screen of the TV monitor saw a foot emerge from the bottom of the bell. But the reception was poor and nothing was observed clearly. The tension of the spectators mounted, and so did their confusion, as they were unable to determine what was happening. One crew member, however, said that he saw two weighted flags dropped on the sea bottom. This was Keller's operations officer, Florian Niggli. Keller himself later stated that he had taken a two-minute swim beyond the range of the cameras.

14

With underwater lights blazing, the bell is returned to the surface. Inside, Keller works over Small, who is dying. Men in the small boat at left are mounting a search for the body of Whittaker. Yet Keller did as he predicted. (BOB JOHNSON PHOTO)

Whatever did happen, one fact is clear and indisputable. The unbelievable depth of one thousand feet had been reached. Both men were still alive.

Keller had obviously returned inside the *Atlantis*. Two figures could be discerned on the TV screen. It was time now to surface. But as those on deck stared at the monitor in horror, Keller and Small slumped over into apparent unconsciousness.

There was no time to figure out what had gone wrong. Nor could help be dispatched to the stricken pair at that great depth. They would have to haul the bell to the surface and hope for a miracle. There was a chance for survival

15

if Keller had had time to close the hatch before he fainted. But if the hatch was still open, there was no chance at all.

As the *Atlantis* was raised, the two safety divers, Anderson and Whittaker, plunged to their maximum depth of two hundred feet and waited for the bell to reach them. When it came, they examined the hatch, which appeared to be closed. The divers went back up to report their findings to the barge crew. But instruments on the *Eureka* indicated that pressure was leaking out of the bell much too rapidly. Something was obviously wrong.

Down went Anderson and Whittaker again to where the *Atlantis* dangled in the sea at two hundred feet. It was an act of heroism on the part of both divers. Their first dive had been a fatiguing experience. Now they had been called upon to do it again under emergency conditions. Anderson, though weary, was in better shape than his partner, Whittaker, who was almost totally fatigued and bleeding from the nose. But Whittaker had insisted on going back, even though he was at the point of exhaustion.

This time the safety men found the trouble. The tip of the swim fin of one of the men inside had lodged itself at the edge of the hatch and prevented it from closing completely. Anderson quickly cut away the flipper and shut the hatch. Then he motioned to Whittaker to swim to the surface and get the bell started up. Whittaker swam off into the misty water above, while Anderson stayed with the bell so he could escort it the rest of the way.

Patiently, Anderson waited for the bell to start rising. When nothing happened, he surfaced to find out why it wasn't moving. On the barge, he discovered the reason. Chris Whittaker had never made it back to the *Eureka*. The courageous diver, his strength gone, had simply vanished into the sea, never to be seen again. It came as a shock to everyone on board, but there was no time for mourning yet. There were still two more lives at stake.

The bell was reeled to the surface. One piece of good news was evident when it arrived there—Keller had regained consciousness. Peter Small, however, still lay there inert. As the bell was rushed to the Long Beach Naval Shipyard, Keller tried desperately to revive his English friend. At the shipyard, the bell, still under pressure, was decompressed according to Keller's tables. Keller emerged shaken but alive. His companion, Peter Small, was dead.

It had been a costly experiment. Two men had paid with their lives. But the overriding fact remained: Keller *had* descended to one thousand feet and had returned alive. His gases had been proven workable, and so had his decompression tables. So the experiment was termed a success—though a tragic one.

16

Saddened by the experience, Keller returned to Switzerland. Though the grim events at Catalina lingered in his mind, he took up his work again. Few on the outside saw the young professor, who became a virtual recluse.

The years passed and Keller's record dive of one thousand feet remained intact. No one came close to the mark he attained; no one even tried, except for certain isolated experiments in pressure tanks.

Then one day Keller emerged smiling from his self-imposed isolation, once again confident and full of plans. He will dive again, he says, this time to work for a full hour at a depth of 1,050 feet, or possibly deeper.

Will he do it? The diving world fervently hopes so, for if he succeeds, a fantastic new world of adventure and achievement awaits the deep-sea diver of the future.

"Probably" inventor Simon Lake. (THE NATIONAL ARCHIVES)

Simon Lake

CAPTAIN NEMO, the bearded master of the submarine *Nautilus,* is one of the great characters in literature. A memorable figure, he appears, of course, in Jules Verne's famous adventure classic, *20,000 Leagues Under the Sea.* Suave and polished, he is a gentleman in every respect. But he is also a fierce fighter, cruel and vengeful when his underwater domain is threatened. Verne's saga of Nemo and his strange craft stirred the imagination of every reader when it was first published in 1869—and still does.

But one young American living in the 1880's was truly inspired by this marvelous tale of conquest and danger in the deep. To him, Captain Nemo was an all-powerful figure with a superior mind, a man after whom he might pattern his own life. And that was just what Simon Lake did. The boy who so admired Captain Nemo grew up to become the man whom history now honors as the developer of the modern submarine.

It was not quite that simple, though Simon Lake, by the age of twenty-five, had invented an improved steering wheel for bicycles, a safety winch, a capping machine, and other devices. He was a natural tinkerer, with the kind of mind that led him to make a thing better than it had been before.

Even in his teens, the submersible vessel fascinated him, so he decided to test certain ideas he had about entrapped air in a vessel. The young inventor paddled his canoe out on the Toms River in New Jersey, then overturned it. Ducking under the water, he poked his head into the air space beneath the canoe, to see how long he could breathe there. Alarmed onlookers from shore

19

saw the capsized, drifting canoe and sadly reported that young Lake had drowned.

He had not, of course, but the incident was an early indication of his character and his methods. Along with unimpeachable honesty, which forced him to test each of his ideas and inventions himself, he was a tireless worker dedicated to solving whatever problem he faced. As to his integrity, Lake once closed down a thriving small business he had built, when he discovered that his associates in the firm were not conducting the business honestly.

The bustling era in which Simon Lake grew to manhood reflected the moods and needs of a growing industrial society. It was also an age of optimism in which everything seemed possible. The idea of the submarine was not new. Robert Fulton, who built and tested his own *Nautilus* in 1800, had been the most notable of the early submarine inventors. Underwater craft had also been used in the American Civil War. But these had been relatively crude and unsophisticated craft. Now a concentrated effort was being made to perfect an undersea vessel that could be used for scientific research as well as warfare. Inventors in many countries began experimenting with new designs for improved submersibles. Two men, however, both of them American, had made the most progress in the race to develop the submarine. The prize that spurred them on was a Navy contract for submarines that each man was anxious to bid on and win.

One was a well-known manufacturer, John Holland, who had been awarded Navy contracts before. He planned to submerge the vessel by the force of propellers and make the submarine itself entirely waterproof. On the surface his vessel would be operated by an engine, underwater by electric motors.

The other leader in the field was Simon Lake. The young inventor had some most unusual ideas about submarines—ideas, in fact, that made many people laugh. It was Lake's plan to submerge his vessel by *sinking* it—by admitting water, just as a sinking ship settles to the bottom.

Both men had experienced some previous success with submersibles on a near-toy level, and so when the Navy announced its plan to contract for a submarine, they both entered bids.

Lake, however, had several problems. High-ranking naval officers clung to firm beliefs about submarines, including the opinion that the entire idea was foolish in the first place. How, for example, could anybody possibly want a boat which could go underwater when the Navy already had the dreadnaughts of the surface fleet? Nevertheless, if a few of the top brass wanted to consider such foolish notions, the rest would "go along."

20

Simon Lake, by then a poor man, points out details on a diagram of his salvage device
Lakso. (WIDE WORLD PHOTO)

21

The submarine, it was finally decided, would be steam-powered, just as every other non-sailing vessel in the Navy was. And worse, for Lake, it certainly would *not* be submerged by admitting water, for this would give the crew little more than a shipwreck to start with. Disappointed, Simon Lake watched from the sidelines as John Holland was awarded the contract. With no influence, no past record of success with Navy contracts, and a crazy idea about how submersibles should work, Simon could almost hear the laughter as he left the Navy boardroom.

Raging at the unfairness of the Navy, he continued to plan his own *Argonaut*. He was sure his theory and techniques were right. His vessel would not only submerge on an even keel (rather than by a series of jerks, as conceived by Holland), but it would also provide surface maneuverability and some comfort for the crew.

For months young Simon Lake struggled to raise the funds he needed to build his own submarine. Meanwhile, he worked on a smaller version.

On January 9, 1895, a young boy slipped away from his home in Oceanic, New Jersey, to go duck hunting. In the early dawn hours, along the banks of the Shrewsbury River, he was seeking a good blind when he halted dead in his tracks. There, ahead of him, bumping gently on the shore, was what appeared to be a three-wheeled coffin. A name painted on the side of this odd-looking contraption proclaimed: *Argonaut, Jr.* The boy ran off to spread the news of his strange discovery.

While a crowd gathered, and newspaper reporters speculated on just what the strange thing was, Simon Lake rowed ashore. The vessel was his submarine—a small-sized version, of course—which had broken free of its moorings during a storm. Not only was it designed to travel on the surface and underwater, Lake explained, but also to crawl for five miles along the bottom on wheels. Most of the people in the crowd smiled politely.

Argonaut, Jr. was about fourteen feet long, five feet from keel to top, flat-bottomed and flat-sided—shaped, in fact, much like an oversized coffin. It had two wheels on the bow and one astern, and was built of layers of wood with a canvas lining. An old soda-fountain pump provided compressed air. A crude crank inside turned the propeller and the wheels. *Argonaut, Jr.* even had an escape trunk in the bottom—a hatch which could be opened to examine the ocean floor. Air pressure inside kept water from entering the vessel.

All in all, the submersible was such an amazing device, particularly since

Simon Lake, the father of the submarine, never lived to see his dream of a cargo-carrying submarine come true. Here he points out his own conception of the vessel to his son, Thomas A. Edison Lake. (THE NATIONAL ARCHIVES)

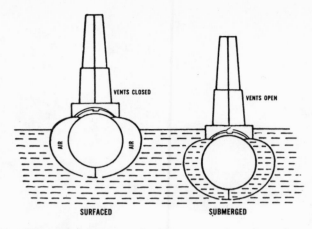

The diagram explains simply the way a submarine submerges. When the vents are opened, water enters the ballast tanks from the bottom, sinking the boat. To surface, air pumps the water back into the sea and the boat floats.

in demonstrations it worked just as Lake had said it would, that at last he was able to raise enough money to build a full-sized *Argonaut.*

Meanwhile, his competitor, John Holland, was going ahead with Navy backing, although there were the problems that always seem to plague a brand-new mechanism. He had instrument troubles, depth-meter problems, inclinometer failures, and other malfunctions, but finally, in March, 1900, his submarine was demonstrated. It was a reasonable success, and Holland's contract was extended to cover five more vessels. It appeared that Holland, not Lake, was on the right course. And in truth, John Holland was responsible in part for the modern submarine.

Simon Lake formed the Lake Torpedo Boat Company, and in 1901 he built the *Protector,* a sixty-five-foot submarine that he was finally allowed to demonstrate to the Navy. It performed flawlessly and a bill was introduced in Congress to purchase five Lake submarines for the Army. Navy lobbyists managed to have the bill defeated, and Lake was heartbroken. He was still convinced that his boat was superior.

Germany, meanwhile, leaned to the Lake theory of submarines, and used his patents freely in their own construction. Perhaps this is one of the reasons why Germany became the first real world power in submarines. Their famous *U-1* was based on Lake's plans, as well as the plans of the French

24

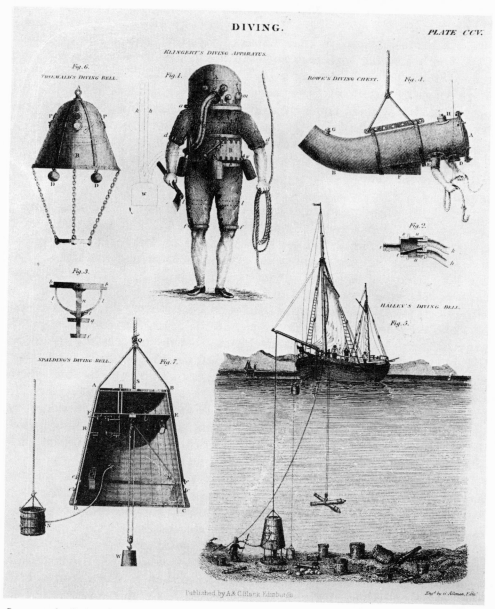

Some early diving devices which Lake studied before forming his own "radical" opinions, most of which were quite correct. (COURTESY SKIN DIVER MAGAZINE)

designer, M. d'Equevilley; and she became the very first of a long line of U-boats.

Unable to convince the United States Navy of the worth of his *Protector,* Lake finally sold her to Russia and took his family there to live while he trained crews. The *Protector* worked so well that Russia had Lake build a fleet of eleven such vessels, and he spent seven years in Europe expanding his operations. He returned home only when he heard that still another bill was before Congress to buy some of his submarines. Congress, apparently, was beginning to see the merit of Lake's approach. The bill was passed, and finally Lake submarines saw service in the United States Navy. In 1912, he built the *Seal,* and in the same year the *Tuna.* More were commissioned, including the famed *S-48.*

But just when his fortunes seemed at their highest point, they turned downward. By then a wealthy man, Simon Lake watched as World War I ended, and along with it, interest in his submarines. He could not convince the government that his vessels could also be used for research and salvage and the carrying of cargo. (The Germans later built their successful cargo-carrying submarine *Deutschland* on Lake's plans.)

A concrete-block company he had founded went bankrupt, and Lake sold his Lake Torpedo Boat Company to pay off the debts. He now had no company and no money. He still had his dreams, though, and a brilliantly inventive mind. Some time before, he had conceived the idea of a tube for salvage work, one wide enough for a man to descend from a ship to the bottom, where Lake had attached a submarine chamber with a bottom hatch. At first he planned to recover what he could from the *Lusitania,* the ship torpedoed by the Germans in 1915. He could not locate the wreck. But even this failure did not dim his spirit. He turned to the hulk of the *Florencia,* a flagship of a Spanish gold armada. Again, the wreck could not be found.

And so, in 1932, Simon Lake designed and built the baby submarine *Explorer* for salvaging treasure. This vessel was connected to a mother ship by air hoses. Lake was sure the *Explorer* would help him recover loot from the *Lusitania,* but once again the wreck's location eluded him.

He returned to the tube concept, and designed and built the *Lakso,* a small compartment at the end of a 115-foot tube that was to be dropped from a surface ship. In the *Lakso,* Lake searched for certain wrecks known to hold treasure or money, but failure plagued him. His dwindling resources faded, and true to his code of strict integrity, he sold his home in Connecticut to satisfy creditors.

26

Still hailed as the father of the modern submarine, Simon Lake died in 1945 without ever seeing his dream of a cargo-carrying submarine come true. But if he were alive today, he would see not only that dream very near reality, but also the fact that today's nuclear submarine, based upon many of his principles, inventions and designs, has become the single most awesome weapon in the world.

Silent, gliding underwater at speeds and depths that are classified secret, the nuclear submarine carries more destructive power—and thus more power for peace—than was expended in both World Wars. Huge cargo-carrying submarines have been designed, and doubtless will become a reality, since storms or surface conditions need not affect their operation.

Simon Lake, a dreamer who worked hard to bring such dreams to reality, can rest easy. He was correct in almost every one of his ideas.

Captain Jacques-Yves Cousteau, the father of self-contained underwater breathing apparatus. (CHAN BUSH PHOTO)

Jacques-Yves Cousteau

WHEN FRANCE fell to the lightning onslaught of Nazi Germany's invading legions in the Second World War, the Italian government set up a headquarters post at Sète, a Mediterranean seaport, to keep itself apprised of plans, situations and significant events pertaining to the war. As time passed, important papers gradually accumulated in the files—papers containing plans and military information that could prove of inestimable value to the Allies.

Understandably, the files were guarded closely around the clock by Italian soldiers. The French underground resistance movement, fully aware of the existence of these files, met to discuss ways and means of gaining access and gathering the intelligence which was available, without alerting the Italians, if possible.

A tall, young naval officer who had been with the French resistance from the first days of the Nazi occupation suggested a solution—an astounding, very dangerous one, to be sure, but inasmuch as the officer had already developed an impressive record of outsmarting the enemy, his colleagues listened.

A short time later, a squad of "Italian" soldiers, led by a hawk-nosed, gangling officer, marched boldly through the entrance of the Italian headquarters. Walking calmly past the guards, the officer opened drawers of the filing cabinets and searched through them as though he were in charge. Then, still maintaining his air of authority, he ordered the guards away; and after photographing every important bit of information at hand, he marched his men out of the building once more.

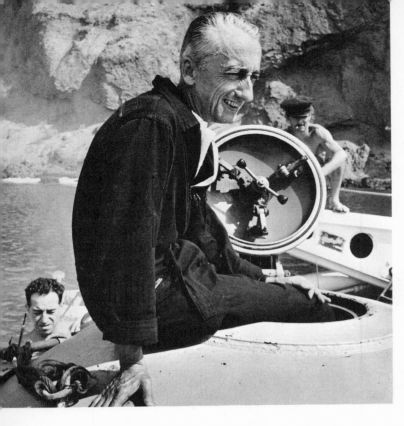

Cousteau poses in the hatch of his diving saucer Denise.
(COURTESY SKIN DIVER MAGAZINE)

This officer was indeed the French naval officer in disguise, and the soldiers accompanying him were Resistance fighters wearing the uniform of the enemy. But of even greater interest, that same naval officer eventually became one of the most renowned men to challenge the ocean, a pioneer in underwater research, and an inventor and designer of underwater equipment. It is his contention that man will one day live for long periods beneath the surface of the ocean. He also envisions a surgical operation that will put *gills* into human throats, to enable men to breathe underwater. His entire life has been one of excitement, adventure, and accomplishment. He is Captain Jacques-Yves Cousteau.

Known as "the first of the menfish," Jacques Cousteau expressed the fascination of underwater adventure best when he declared, "From birth [man] carries the weight of gravity on his shoulders. He is bolted to earth. But man has only to sink beneath the surface and he is free. Buoyed by water, he can fly in any direction—up, down, sideways—by merely flipping his hand. Underwater, man becomes an archangel."

Yet, before Cousteau became the father of modern skin diving, he

30

dreamed most of becoming an aviator in the French Air Force. This, and a love for fast cars, led him at first through hardship and pain, and then finally into oceanography.

Born in June, 1910, in Saint-André-de-Cubzac near Bordeaux in France, young Jacques' home was in Paris, when he wasn't traveling with his father, a lawyer. During one trip he spent a year in the United States, in New York City. He was ten years old then, and showed a flair for adventure even at that age, yet nobody suspected that he would eventually become one of the best known Frenchmen in the annals of the sea.

Future renown seemed particularly doubtful when poor health appeared to be leading toward some lackluster calling. A victim of chronic enteritis and anemia during his adolescence, Cousteau was advised by his doctors to avoid all strenuous activity for the rest of his life.

In reviewing Cousteau's amazing career, it is difficult to imagine that he could *ever* have been inactive. Today, however, the debilitating effects of

Denise *is lowered over the stern of Cousteau's research vessel* Calypso.

(COURTESY SKIN DIVER MAGAZINE)

Cousteau's earlier years are evident in his face and body. He is a gnarled, thin shadow of a man, hollow-cheeked and with a very prominent nose. Physically he appears carved and chiseled from incredibly strong but very thin stock. Veins stand out on his hands and forehead. His large eyes are arresting, crinkling at one moment into humor and narrowing at another into intent interest. He is polite, but haughty.

Young Cousteau graduated from Stanislas Academy in Paris and enrolled at the Naval Academy at Brest, his eyes focused on the sky. To be a pilot was all he desired. Honor-ranked as the second highest man in his class, he entered the fleet's air school. Diving beneath the sea was then of no particular concern to him, except as a sport.

Then, one dark night, shortly before the end of his course at the flying school, he was driving along a mountain road in his father's Salmson sports car. Life was good and he was happy. But suddenly life, like the road, took a new turn.

The lights flickered out and the sharply winding road could no longer be seen. Cousteau was traveling fast. Fighting the wheel, he tried to guess, but guessed wrong. The car swerved wildly out of control, left the road, and rolled over several times. In the smoking wreckage, Cousteau felt waves of pain. His left arm was shattered; his right, paralyzed.

At the hospital where the young man was taken after being found, doctors insisted his left arm would have to be amputated.

Jacques-Yves Cousteau was adamant with the medical authorities. "You are the owner of your own body," he argued, and refused to allow them to cut off his arm, though it was broken almost beyond repair. The doctors thereupon set it as best they could, and a long period of recuperation began.

Flying was no longer possible, and so Cousteau's career as an airman was over before it had really begun. He was still an officer in the French Navy, but his arms were almost useless. Long months of struggle followed, and only Cousteau believed that he could regain full use of his injured limbs. Gradually he conquered the paralysis, and when he was stationed at the Toulon Naval Base during the mid-thirties, he took to swimming to strengthen his weak arms. He met another officer, Phillippe Tailliez, and a civilian, Frederic Dumas, and the three men began to dive and hunt underwater.

A whole new world opened up for Jacques Cousteau . . . the underwater world. He became an avid diver. Every spare moment was spent in the clear blue waters of the Mediterranean, diving, spearfishing, and marveling at the wondrous things to be seen. But there was, for him, a frustrating limitation of his activities. He could not dive deep enough, nor stay under long enough. And so began his experiments which radically changed the life not only of Cousteau, but of millions of undersea sportsmen and adventurers since then.

Cousteau began to work with a brilliant young French engineer, Émile Gagnan. The two men wanted a device which would provide measured amounts of air to a diver from compressed air tanks, and allow him to swim deep and stay under for long intervals of time. The Germans then occupied France and their top scientists were working on similar technological concepts. But the Germans paid little attention to the two nondescript Frenchmen who, under their very noses, daily headed for the beach with their bottles and regulators. Had they done so, the course of the war might have changed, for the Germans were also looking into underwater breathing methods which would allow frogmen to penetrate harbors and destroy warships, bridges or shipping facilities.

The inflatable saucer carrier Amphitrite, *designed by Cousteau.*
(COURTESY SKIN DIVER MAGAZINE)

At first Cousteau experimented with single cylinders of compressed air that had a valve to regulate the flow of air to his mouth, but the apparatus was good only for shallow dives of short duration. Cousteau then designed a re-breathing unit which used pure oxygen and forced his exhalations through a canister of soda lime for purification. The device produced violent convulsions, for Cousteau did not know then that oxygen, under the pressures of diving, is poisonous to the human system. It nearly cost him his life before he returned to air-regulating techniques, rather than oxygen re-breathing units.

Cousteau and Gagnan then made a discovery. They used an automatic regulator designed for automobile engines and modified it to feed air to a diver. Early in 1943, Cousteau tested the unit in the river Marne just outside Paris. It consisted of three cylinders of compressed air, the regulator (about the size of an alarm clock), two tubes for intake and exhaust, the harness, and straps. The regulator was designed to assure a flow of air, regardless of the water pressure. In diving the air inside the lungs must be of the same pressure as the water outside or the body will be crushed.

Cousteau's companions, Dumas, Tailliez and Gagnan, watched anxiously from the shore. His wife Simone swam on the surface overhead, peering down through a face mask and breathing through a snorkel tube. At first the regula-tor worked well only with the diver in a horizontal position, and that was all. Minor modifications were made and the device retested. Cousteau glided and soared underwater, every movement a picture of grace. He felt a surge of triumph.

The Aqua-Lung was perfect!

Cousteau continued his experiments with underwater breathing and underwater motion-picture making, and produced the movie *Sunken Ships* from spliced-together film strips while the Germans were still in France. He studied the strange "drunkenness" produced by an oversaturation of nitrogen in the blood, and named it "rapture of the deep."

Finally, the German occupation forces were driven out of France, and Cousteau applied to the French government for funds and permission to con-tinue his research. A very persuasive man, he was granted this request, and for a time Cousteau, Tailliez and Dumas used themselves as human guinea pigs in various experiments. They once subjected themselves to underwater explosions to discover the effects such detonations would have upon divers. They removed mines and torpedoes from the hulls of ships and from harbors. They tested the Aqua-Lung to see if it could be adapted for use as an escape apparatus from sunken submarines.

Jacques-Yves Cousteau receives a gold medal from President Kennedy for his ocean-ographic work. (COURTESY NATIONAL GEOGRAPHIC SOCIETY)

Eventually the team, which had become known as the Undersea Research Group (or G.E.R.S., for *Groupe d'Études et de Recherches Sous-Marines*), acquired an ocean-going tender, the *Elie-Monnier*, and with it they extended their activities.

Cousteau took a leave of absence from the French Navy to conduct oceanographic work aboard the *Calypso*, a 360-ton, 141-foot converted mine-sweeper which served as a floating base of operations.

Cousteau received the coveted gold "Oscar," Hollywood's highest award, for his impressive motion picture, *The Silent World*. It was based on his book, a best-seller that has sold over five million copies and is still going strong. The motion picture also won the highest award at the Cannes Film Festival, the Grand Prix. More recently, Cousteau's films have been shown to fascinated viewers on television.

Motion-picture photography underwater is difficult enough at best, but for a time Cousteau and his crew had more than their share of problems with a grouper fish they had named Ulysses. Filming at beautiful Assumption Reef, a virgin wilderness in the tropical sea off Assumption Island in the Indian Ocean, the diving crew befriended the fat old three-foot fish, and it became their pet. As filming went on, though, Ulysses became an uninhibited pet, and then a mischievous one. At first he would snap tidbits from the divers' hands, but as he became more sure of himself he would eat an entire bag of food at one gulp, even though it was intended for other fish.

And he would constantly get in the way of the camera, almost as though he knew what was happening, dogging the heels of the divers, bumping them, and ruining scenes. They could not kill their friend, in spite of the damage he was doing, and they did not feel right in driving him from his own home ground, yet he became even more persistent.

Finally the answer occurred to the divers. "Lower the shark cage!" they ordered, referring to a steel-barred cage which was always on the deck of the *Calypso,* ready to be lowered to give divers instant protection from any sharks that might stray into the area.

Crewmen on deck hurried to the task, fearing momentarily for the divers below.

"No, there are no sharks," the divers assured them, "but we need the cage anyhow."

The cage was lowered, Ulysses was enticed into it with food, and there the pesky old fish remained, in "jail," to be fed through the bars until filming was finished. When the divers opened the door to the cage, Ulysses refused to leave his new home, and had to be driven from it to freedom.

Jacques-Yves Cousteau has a consuming interest in wrecks, particularly ancient wrecks. His company has discovered and conducted salvage work aboard many of them. On the floor of the Mediterranean, he found the remains of a Greek freighter which had gone down over two thousand years before. Cousteau brought up over eight thousand amphoras (earthenware jars used for storage in ancient times) and many thousands of dishes, bowls, cups and flasks.

"A dead ship is the house of tremendous life," says Cousteau. "The mixture of life and death is mysterious, even religious. [There is] a sense of peace and mood that you feel on entering a cathedral."

One of his greatest accomplishments came on July 29, 1956, when he anchored his research ship *Calypso* in 25,000 feet of water off the Ivory Coast

Jacques Cousteau in a moment of relaxation. (CHAN BUSH PHOTO)

of Africa. Coming to a halt over the tremendously deep Romanche Trench, the ship's thin nylon anchor cable was paid out until the anchor bit into the bottom. It was the deepest anchorage ever achieved by man.

In the Romanche Trench, Cousteau used a submersible camera designed and built by Professor Harold E. Edgerton, of the Massachusetts Institute of Technology, to take sharp, clear pictures of the ocean floor at a depth of 24,600 feet, more than a half-mile deeper than man had ever photographed it before.

Cousteau's accomplishments go on and on. He designed and built *Denise,* an odd underwater vehicle which can carry two observers to a depth of more than a thousand feet. Unlike the usual uncontrolled bathysphere, which merely hangs by a cable from a mother ship, *Denise* is steerable and free of connections to her surface tender. Basically, she is a steel ball about six and a half feet across and five feet deep, or slightly saucer-shaped. Around this inner pressure hull are packed the motor, jet pump and batteries, all enclosed in fiberglass streamlined fairings, which give *Denise* her true saucer shape. In front are viewing ports. From inside, the occupants may steer the rudderless craft by aiming jets of water, so she can travel up, down or sideways in this manner. A hydraulically operated claw enables the men inside to examine sea-bottom samples at close range by picking them up and bringing them close to a viewing port.

Then Cousteau designed and built an air-filled rubber boat to carry *Denise,* which he named *Amphitrite. Denise* is customarily carried on the stern of the *Calypso,* but with a deflatable, foldable support craft she can be flown conveniently to any location in the world.

Cousteau staged a remarkable demonstration of aquatic control shortly after *Denise* was built. Wearing underwater breathing apparatus and diving to the bottom, he swam about, up and down, two assistants inside maneuvering *Denise* into matching his every move. She followed her builder, according to fond observers, "like a little puppy dog." He has most recently built and tested twin one-man submersibles with even greater range and maneuverability.

Cousteau worked on experiments with the *Trieste,* the bathyscaph which eventually penetrated to the deepest ocean trench. He designed the Westinghouse *Deepstar* submersible, a seven-ton hydrodynamically shaped vessel capable of reaching a depth of 12,000 feet and maneuvering freely there with a three-man crew. He also founded the flourishing French Undersea Research Center at Marseilles.

Finally, in 1956, Cousteau retired from the French Navy with the rank of Capitaine de Corvette to assume the directorship of the Oceanographic Museum at Monaco. In 1959 he was elected president of the World Underwater Federation.

Recently Cousteau conceived, developed and managed the French experiments in underwater living similar to the Sealab projects of the United States. Once, when the two nations were independently conducting simultaneous underwater projects, a telephone connection was arranged between the American aquanauts of Sealab II, off the coast of Southern California, and the French aquanauts. It was humorous, and rather eerie, to hear men speaking from deep ocean habitats across the world from each other, particularly in the high-pitched, squeaky "Donald Duck" voices caused by the helium of their atmospheres.

Cousteau also experimented with concrete "apartment houses" for fish and other marine creatures, attempting to breed them in much the same manner as farm animals. The sea eventually will provide much more of the food for the world, and he feels that this preliminary work is most necessary. On his drawing boards are newer and better submersibles for the peaceful invasion of deep ocean trenches.

Cousteau certainly would have become a great airman for France, but the sports car accident he suffered was a fortunate one for oceanographers (and for Cousteau, too, since nearly every one of his classmates who went on to become pilots were killed in World War II). The accident led Cousteau into an outstanding career of ocean study and conquest.

Perhaps Cousteau and many other scientists are correct in their belief in the feasibility of a surgical operation which will put gills into a man's throat. Still in the future, this operation, if carried to a successful conclusion, would enable man to swim free of all encumbrances and breathe water like a fish. Cousteau himself has volunteered as a subject when the studies are complete.

Then the father of scuba diving, and the entire oceanographic world, will have taken a gigantic step into the future.

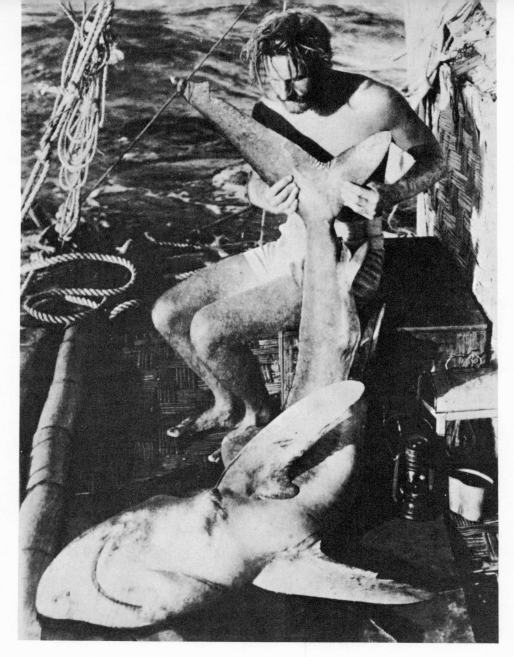

Thor Heyerdahl examines a shark during the strange voyage of Kon-Tiki.

Thor Heyerdahl

THE MAN and his wife sat before a dancing fire, on the beach of a quiet, peaceful island in the South Pacific. The setting was idyllic. The time was the late 1930's, and the two were enjoying a holiday among the island people they loved.

They did not suspect that the old man on the other side of the fire, who was telling a story in the beautiful language of the Polynesians, would lead the husband into one of the most hazardous adventures in any man's life.

But it was easy for the imagination of explorer, author, and ethnologist Thor Heyerdahl to become excited about a new theory. Slender, handsome, Heyerdahl had led a life of travel and adventure which might have made any man envy him.

The native talked on about his man-god ancestors, who they were, their fame while living, and where they had gone. But he did not know for certain where his ancestors had come from. Perhaps, as the legend had it, they had traveled from a country beyond the sea to the east, riding the *Pae-Pae* (raft).

Heyerdahl considered the old man's words carefully, aware that anthropologists had supposedly "pinned down" the land from which the South Sea Islanders had emigrated, if not precisely, at least to each individual researcher's satisfaction. Some said China, others insisted upon India, and still others leaned to the theory that the Islanders' ancestors had originally come from Japan, Arabia, or the "lost continent" of Atlantis, or even from Heyerdahl's own Norway. But to the east was South America, more than four thousand

41

uncharted sea miles away. Could the god Tiki actually have come from there?

Impossible, and yet Heyerdahl mentally checked off in his mind the similarities between island cultures and certain indications of a lost culture he had studied in Peru. It was true that once, before the records of man, a civilization had flourished in the Peruvian mountains. But they had abruptly disappeared, almost as if . . . as if swallowed up by the sea.

The thought hit Heyerdahl's imagination. What if the ancient Peruvian civilization, told in tales by the Inca Indians before their own disappearance, had *not* been slaughtered in battle to the last man, woman and child, but rather had been driven into the sea? Perhaps Tiki had led his people toward the setting sun (he *was* looked upon as the sun god) to escape the terror of the Inca.

It seemed incredible that such an ancient civilization could have traveled thousands of miles through violent ocean storms without modern ships, supplies and navigational aids, yet, the more Thor Heyerdahl considered it, the more he believed it to be possible.

The crew of the Kon-Tiki. *Left to right, Thor Heyerdahl, Bengt Danielsson, Erik Hesselberg, Torstein Raaby, Herman Watzinger, and Knut Haugland.* (WIDE WORLD PHOTO)

When he returned to Norway, Heyerdahl went back to his study of primitive civilizations, but the Second World War came along and he served his country against the occupying Nazis. Ten years later, the old native's words still in his memory, he turned once again to his fascinating conjecture. The experts he talked to disagreed forcefully with his theory, however, saying it was almost heresy to suggest that island culture and South American culture had intermingled. In spite of certain similarities, including huge stone statues on Easter Island, also in mid-Pacific, it was contrary to what every scientific authority had come to believe. How could unsophisticated natives with no knowledge of the sea travel from South America to the Pacific islands? It was unthinkable . . . and yet Heyerdahl had a strong hunch that it *could* have happened.

There remained but one way to prove his theory, a dangerous, almost foolhardy, way. He would build a raft that would conform to the most ancient plans he could find, and then launch it from Peru with only himself and a carefully chosen crew aboard, allowing it to drift on winds and currents. For taking this calculated risk, the adventurers might all suffer inglorious defeat and perhaps death by being hurled ashore along South America, or perhaps drift off into the ocean, never to be heard from again. If Heyerdahl's theory was right, though, they would make their way to the islands of the Polynesians. He was now convinced that the sun god Tiki had been driven from Peru by the Incas and had taken to the sea to search for a new land. Man changes with the ages, but ocean currents and winds remain almost constant.

It was not an easy project. He was greeted at the very outset with resistance and laughter. Yet, with the help of his first volunteer, Herman Watzinger, he found a group of men who thought as he did and were willing to back him financially. From the United States Government he obtained survival equipment, "just in case." Norwegians Knut Haugland, Torstein Raaby and Erik Hesselberg, and finally, Swedish-born Bengt Danielsson, were chosen for the remainder of the crew.

The construction of the raft began in the harbor of the naval base at Lima, Peru. Abiding by ancient traditions and customs, Heyerdahl named each of the twelve giant balsa logs he used after a legendary Polynesian figure: *Ku, Kane, Kama, Ilo, Mauri, Ra, Rangi, Papa, Tranga, Kura, Kukara* and *Hiti.*

Sea experts pointed out that balsa was a highly porous wood, and warned that the raft would sink after only a few days, when the logs became water-soaked. Heyerdahl argued ineffectually that the sap in the wood would prevent water from entering deep into the pores. (Later, in fact, water-soaked chunks of wood from the raft did indeed sink quickly, portending a dim future for the project.)

In honor of the Polynesian god in whose steps they hoped they were following, Heyerdahl christened the raft *Kon-Tiki,* and on April 28, 1947, the amazing voyage began. Not a wire nor a spike nor a piece of iron or steel had been used to lash *Kon-Tiki* together. She was forty-five feet long at her centerline, and tapered to shorter thirty-foot logs at each side. This length accounted for nine of the logs; three others were cross-lashed to give the raft rigidity. A sail of native material bearing the bearded face of Kon-Tiki was mounted on a cross-lashed mast of iron-hard mangrove wood, and a long steering oar projected astern.

The Humboldt Current sweeps in an icy stream northward along the coast of South America, and *Kon-Tiki* was soon into it. But almost immediately storms tore at the raft and made steering almost impossible. The current swept them on toward the treacherous reefs of the Galapagos Islands off Ecuador. Heyerdahl pondered this development. Either *Kon-Tiki* would turn westward toward the open ocean, or she would crash to her destruction far from where he had thought she would go.

The ocean of ancient times had certainly been the master of Tiki's craft and so it would also direct this one. Proof of the validity of Heyerdahl's theory might not await days and weeks on the open ocean. It might become evident on the rocks of the Galapagos Islands.

Gradually, however, the small circles on the chart which was kept by Hesselberg began to swing in a westerly direction as day-by-day positions were noted. The Humboldt Current was carrying them out into the open sea, away from South America and toward—not a man aboard *Kon-Tiki* knew for sure.

It was at this time that the outer layers of the balsa logs became waterlogged, and small chips came off, promptly sinking out of sight. Each man noting this kept the disconcerting discovery to himself. The dramatic voyage went on. By May 10, traveling northwest, *Kon-Tiki* came closest to the equator, and then began to drift in a southwesterly direction.

The Pacific islands of Tiki were southwest.

In his log, Heyerdahl noted a fact which no one had considered before the trip. Each of the huge logs forming the hull of *Kon-Tiki* was moving independently to form a gently undulating deck. But more important, the ropes that tied the logs together were wearing into the logs, and not being chafed apart by them as the voyagers had been warned might happen. If, instead of

44

the ropes, the men had used chains or cables, as they had considered doing, the logs would certainly have been sawed apart by the constant movement. Once again, a portent of success became apparent. The god Tiki would surely not have had cables or chains available. He, too, would have had to use the ropes.

Kon-Tiki rode on, day after day, accepting gracefully whatever the stormy ocean threw at her, lumbering up and then sliding down the sides of huge waves. The raft proved to be extremely seaworthy. Water washing onto the deck would merely run out between the logs before it had a chance to do any damage. The thatchwork cabin was completely dry almost all the time.

Still, between storms and calms, the voyage was ever-changing and exciting. Sharks, whales, dolphins, and pilot fish adopted the raft, resting beneath its protective bulk and following it for weeks. At night, crewmen could look

Thor Heyerdahl, leader of the Kon-Tiki *expedition, selects survival gear provided by the U.S. Government before his amazing voyage across the ocean on a raft.*

(WIDE WORLD PHOTO)

down into the phosphorescent sea through chinks in the deck, and see the huge eyes of underwater creatures staring up at the odd assembly of logs overhead. Each morning the cook for the day would collect flying fish which had landed on deck, and other marine creatures, and soon the tempting aroma of breakfast would wake the others. The men once sighted a giant whale shark, said to be the largest living fish, as it ventured to within a few feet of the raft for an examination. Finally it dismissed *Kon-Tiki* as harmless and drifted back down into the blue depths.

Another time the crew rescued a huge, helpless sea turtle which was being attacked by fish, though the rescue operation was intended to land the turtle in an even more hazardous position—in the cooking pot. The turtle escaped, however, and a new and dangerous aspect of raft life became evident. Some equipment had gone overboard during the rescue. It led to a harsh rule aboard:

"Once overboard, *always* overboard."

It was impossible to turn the lumbering raft, and at the same time it was drifting fast enough forward to escape any swimmer. If a man fell overboard, he would be left behind as the raft drifted farther away from him. Stringent safety rules were adopted, one of which was that safety ropes would be worn around the waist of the steersman.

Even so, a mishap did occur. With the fate of the crew's parrot still fresh in their minds (it had fallen overboard, and could not be rescued), Herman Watzinger attempted to grab a sleeping bag which was going over the side in a storm, and went overboard himself. Immediately he drifted astern.

He tried to grab the end of the steering oar, but it slipped from his grasp. The raft, driven even faster by the storm, moved steadily away from Watzinger, while the noise of the raging sea drowned out his cries.

"Man overboard!" came a call at last, though by then Watzinger was already well astern. The lifesaving gear which was tossed out to him fell short of his reach. In the howling wind, he drifted even farther astern, until he could be seen only when the waves brought him up into view.

Throwing caution to the screaming wind, Knut Haugland plunged into the turbulent water and struck out toward Watzinger. In his arms he held a life belt with a line attached. Gradually the two bobbing heads drew closer together until they met. Then the men on the raft hauled on the line with all their might.

Exhausted from their struggle, the two men were finally pulled aboard the raft. Beneath them, in the sea, as if to add extra, unnecessary drama, the

Kon-Tiki *sails from Callao, Peru, at the very beginning of its long voyage. According to ancient tradition, the face of the god Tiki has been painted on the sail.*

(WIDE WORLD PHOTO)

huge shadow of an unknown marine creature drifted back into the depths. In its jaws was the sleeping bag which had precipitated the near-tragedy.

By July 3, the raft was drifting steadily southwest by means of ocean currents and winds. Far beyond the halfway point along their estimated 4,300-

47

nautical-mile journey, the men of the *Kon-Tiki* were in high spirits. The sea was providing motive power and fine food. They ate and enjoyed not only fresh fish, but also plankton, the microscopic organism of the ocean. They learned to drink a certain amount of ocean water, as well as the fresh water they carried, with no ill effects and, in some cases, with beneficial results.

So they drifted on, with Heyerdahl as the chief log-keeper, Danielsson as the chief steward in charge of supplies, Watzinger as the meterologist and hydrographic expert, Haugland and Raaby as radiomen (a wireless transmitter and receiver was aboard and sometimes functioned phenomenally), and

After the successful voyage, the raft is loaded aboard a ship for return home and an exhibition tour. (WIDE WORLD PHOTO)

Hesselberg as navigator. The difficult or dull duties, such as steering and cooking, were divided equally among the men.

On July 30, early in the morning, Watzinger climbed the stubby cross-masts for a sighting. Quietly he stared at the horizon, then he climbed back down and entered the cabin where the others were sleeping. Shaking Heyerdahl by the leg, he spoke:

"Come out and have a look at your island."

Ahead, in the dim mists, was a pencil-thin outline of land. They had reached their goal, and proven what they had set out to prove, for the land was the island of Pukapuka, outermost of the Tuamotu group of islands. They stared, almost in disbelief, after their long weeks at sea.

Kon-Tiki, however, drifted past Pukapuka, and the island finally faded far astern. But the crew was no longer concerned, since thousands of such islands dotted the sea ahead, and they cared little which one their faithful raft would select.

The second landfall was the island of Angatau, but though some natives met them offshore to help guide the raft through treacherous reefs, a landing was rejected as being too dangerous. Gradually the wind pushed them back to sea. Knut Haugland was almost left behind, for he had gone ashore to recruit additional manpower to help pull the raft into the lagoon.

Finally, on the 101st day at sea, an island appeared dead ahead. It was ringed by a cruel coral reef, where the water boomed and boiled over into a calm lagoon. It was obviously the destination *Kon-Tiki* had chosen, for they were driven straight into the breakers. A wild ride over the reef, which damaged the raft severely and nearly cost the lives of the crew, ended in the peaceful lagoon. Stretched out on the sand, safe and secure, the crew named the island Kon-Tiki.

The voyage was over. The theory was proven to Heyerdahl's satisfaction, and to the satisfaction of several previously skeptical scientists. Kon-Tiki and his people could indeed have drifted from Peru to the South Pacific Islands.

In a short time the crew was discovered and warmly welcomed by the natives. There were feasts and celebrations, after the word spread that the adventurers had come from across the sea on a *Pae-Pae,* just as the gods once had done. Each man in the crew was elevated to god status and was given a suitable native name. *Kon-Tiki* was rescued from the reef, repaired, and finally towed by motor launch to Tahiti, where more celebrations and new names and honors awaited the crew.

It was an idyllic end to a successful, if hazardous, voyage, a voyage which

Thor Heyerdahl perches atop one of the mysterious head statues on Easter Island while members of the expedition measure its size. (WIDE WORLD PHOTO)

50

added significant knowledge to the study of primitives of South America and Polynesia, and for which Heyerdahl and his crew have since received international recognition.

Thor Heyerdahl wrote a fascinating book, *Kon-Tiki,* full of the adventure and excitement of the strange voyage, which became a best seller. Unable to rest on his laurels, as most men would, he returned again to the mid-Pacific to investigate the stone statues on Easter Island for another possible connection between Peru and Polynesia. About this adventure he wrote still another fine book called *Aku-Aku.*

Today, as one of the most daring of all the men who challenge the sea, he still seeks adventure. If Thor Heyerdahl's past life is an indication, he will certainly find it.

Auguste Piccard (right) describes his descent in his bathyscaph to reporters, before turning over command to his son Jacques (center). (WIDE WORLD PHOTO)

Auguste and Jacques Piccard

OUTSIDE, THROUGH the thick, cone-shaped porthole, the sea was as black as midnight. Except for her own lamps, not a glimmer of light penetrated to the great depth of the odd vessel. Down it sank, ever deeper, almost like a lost ship. The tremendous pressure of the water tried to crush the craft, but it held firm.

Inside the spherical cabin, beneath a huge gasoline-filled float, two men waited tensely. Soon, they knew, they were bound to reach the sea floor. With nothing to see outside, both men stared at the sonic depth finder, as if to induce thereby some indication of proximity to the bottom, but without immediate effect.

Deeper still sank the bathyscaph *Trieste* into the Mariana Trench, off Guam Island in the South Pacific Ocean. The year was 1960. After a diligent search for the deepest point in the oceans of the world, far deeper than any man had ever thought of penetrating before, the Challenger Deep of the Mariana Trench had been found. Soundings had marked a depth of 5,966 fathoms—nearly 35,800 feet. If Mount Everest, the mightiest mountain in the world, could be physically transplanted to this monstrous gash on the ocean floor, its peak would still be more than six thousand feet below the surface!

At the bottom the craft would be subjected to three thousand *tons* of pressure. Even if the steel sphere didn't collapse, and it had been built to allow even greater calculated pressures, the two men within it could be killed instantly by merely a pinpoint leak. Water, streaking in through even a minuscule opening, would enter with the force of a bullet.

53

Jacques Piccard in the conning tower of the amazing bathyscaph Trieste. (U.S. NAVY PHOTO)

But all was going well. Far above on the surface the United States Navy's ocean-going tugboat *Wandank* awaited developments, and standing off to assist was the destroyer escort *Lewis*. Below, *Trieste* sank deeper, past 31,000 feet, then 32,000 feet. Still, the sonic depth finder did not record.

Could the previous measurements have been wrong? The two men glanced at each other. Perhaps they were dropping to a new and unknown depth. The "bottom" might very well be without substance, a soft fluid mud which would not show up on the *Trieste*'s instruments, and into which the bathyscaph might be sinking inescapably.

Navy Lieutenant Don Walsh, a handsome young submarine officer, and a willing volunteer on the mission, glanced across at his companion and grinned. They were committed to the dangerous dive, and worry wouldn't

54

help. To relieve the tension, he shifted slightly, attempting to untangle his own legs from those of his fellow scientist in the confining steel sphere. It was not easy, for his pilot on the plunge was the six-foot-seven-inch Swiss scientist Jacques Piccard, a daring oceanographer of world renown. Piccard —a name quickly associated with going the highest, or the deepest, or the most hazardous way, always with scientific conquest the ultimate goal.

Jacques Piccard was the son of Auguste Piccard, a physicist of great courage. It had been Auguste who, determined to study high-velocity particles from outer space at closer range, first climbed a high mountain and then, finding it not nearly high enough, built an airtight gondola which, attached to a large balloon, carried him to 53,000 feet, an incredible height in 1932. Auguste then conceived a similar "balloon" float which would carry a man into the chasms of the ocean, and, with his son Jacques, built just such a vessel.

These two men have been deeper in the ocean than any other men in history. Navy Lt.
Don Walsh (left) and Jacques Piccard study a fitting for use on the Trieste.

(U.S. NAVY PHOTO)

Jacques Piccard (left) and Lt. Don Walsh on the deck of the Trieste *before its epic dive.*

A professor of physics at the University of Brussels and twin brother of the noted aeronautical engineer-chemist, Jean Piccard, who also made a stratospheric balloon ascent to an altitude of 57,000 feet, Auguste Piccard had the searching mind of a true scientist and the courage to pursue his theories. To his son, Jacques, he gave the same qualities.

So the two men, father and son, invented, designed, and built the first bathyscaph in the world, a deep submersible vessel not attached to a surface ship by cable. The craft was called the *FNRS-2,* since the high altitude balloon had been designated the *FNRS.* The submersible vessel had been foremost in the mind of Auguste Piccard for many years, and in 1948 it finally made its first successful unmanned dive to a depth of 4,800 feet. Eventually the *FNRS-2* was sold to the French Navy and rebuilt (with the Piccards' help) as the *FNRS-3*. But meanwhile, Auguste and his son were developing plans for still another bathyscaph, one capable of going to the deepest point in all the oceans. She would be called the *Trieste*.

In September, 1953, off Castellammare in the Gulf of Naples, the *Trieste,* with Auguste and Jacques Piccard aboard, made her first dive. Though the depth was only five fathoms, or thirty feet, the basic concept was proven to be correct and practicable.

The bathyscaph, the invention of the Piccards, functions more like a balloon than a deep-diving vessel. The men are housed in a steel, watertight sphere beneath the float, the important component of the craft. The float is filled with gasoline before a dive and, as it is then lighter than water, it keeps the craft buoyant. Ballast containers fore and aft in the float are filled with iron shot pellets. An almost perfect neutral buoyancy is thereby created. The men enter the sphere through an access tube and close the hatch; then they operate the valves which flood air tanks in the gasoline-filled float with water. This extra weight makes the bathyscaph descend.

The four men most responsible for the deep dive known as Project Nekton. Left to right, pilot Jacques Piccard, observer Lt. Don Walsh, scientist-in-charge Dr. Andreas B. Rechnitzer, observer Lt. Larry Shumaker. (U.S. NAVY PHOTO)

As it drifts slowly downward, the sphere is strong enough to resist the pressure of the ocean. Valves in the float let sea water flow in as the pressure increases, but the water and gasoline do not mix, so the float maintains the same pressure inside and out, and does not collapse. Controls allow the men to release ballast at any time, which slows the descent or even causes the bathyscaph to rise again if enough of the iron shot is dropped. This can be done by turning off an electro-magnet which holds the shot in place. The crew can also release the gasoline in the float and make the craft sink more rapidly.

If something should go wrong, all of the iron shot pellets and their containers can be discarded in an instant. They are dropped automatically if the power in the craft should fail. In such an event, the vessel returns to the surface.

Suspended beneath the bathyscaph is a long chain which helps slow descent as the vessel nears the bottom, for the weight of the chain is gradually reduced as it slacks off on the sea floor, making the bathyscaph itself lighter.

So precise are these changes in weight that the bathyscaph always approaches the bottom with gentle deliberation until it pauses, almost on tiptoe, like a dancer, inches away. There it has a certain maneuvering ability derived from propellers driven by electric motors.

When the observers are ready to return to the surface, the ballast is released and the craft starts its ascent. As pressure is reduced on the float, the gasoline inside forces water back out and everything is once again balanced and slightly buoyant.

Nine years before his death in 1962, Auguste Piccard, then an old man with a leonine mane of white hair, made a dive in the *Trieste* to a depth of 10,300 feet.

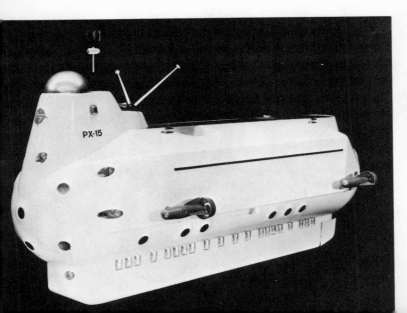

Jacques Piccard's latest project is the PX-15, a deep drifting submersible. This is a scale model of the vehicle which is currently under construction. (GRUMMAN AVIATION ENGINEERING CORP. PHOTO)

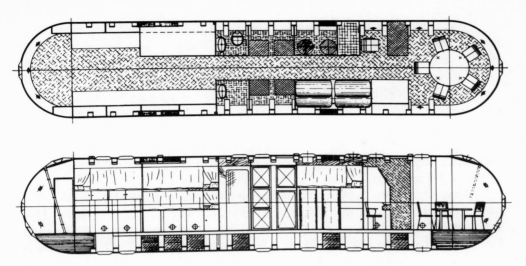

An inboard profile of the PX-15, showing layout of equipment and facilities.
(GRUMMAN AVIATION ENGINEERING CORP. PHOTO)

On October 1, 1953, Auguste turned over the job of pilot of the *Trieste* to his son Jacques. With the help of his son, he had planned her, built her, and tested her at a crushing depth. It became the son's job to carry on.

And carry on Jacques did. Many dives were made, with leading scientists of the world as observers. Finally, the United States Navy expressed an interest in the bathyscaph, and her future in the abysses was assured, for with the support of the Navy came funds for modifications and extended operations. The Navy purchased the *Trieste*, with Jacques Piccard contracted as pilot and technical director.

American oceanographers of the caliber of Dr. Andreas Rechnitzer, Dr. Robert Dill, and Dr. Robert Dietz entered the spherical cabin and plunged to new record depths. The pilot was always Jacques Piccard, now the master of the *Trieste*. On November 15, 1959, in an area south of Guam, Piccard and Rechnitzer, as scientist-in-charge, plunged to 18,150 feet. No man had ever gone deeper into the ocean.

While on the bottom, Rechnitzer described a strange creature which resembled a Pharaoh's cap, a worm-like creature with wings, and a "beautiful" sight. Piccard stared spellbound through the tiny port at the strange animal never before seen by man as Rechnitzer rapidly took pictures and related his observations on a tape recorder.

59

Back on the surface, with final test dives almost completed, every man turned his thoughts to Project Nekton, the Navy's name for the deepest dive in history, to take place at the Challenger Deep of the Mariana Trench.

Only one test dive remained, and on January 8, 1960, it was made into the Nero Deep of the South Pacific Ocean. The pilot was Jacques Piccard; the observer, Lieutenant Don Walsh. The depth reached was an astounding 23,000 feet!

So only the Challenger Deep remained. Preparations were made, and a crew selected. It would, according to the Navy, be Project Director Rechnitzer and Lieutenant Walsh for the ultimate dive.

Jacques Piccard protested. His father had invented the craft, he pointed out, and he had helped to build her. That didn't matter, said the Navy. This was to be a Navy mission, and so a naval officer and a naval civilian would make the dive. Piccard argued, for he wanted to pilot the *Trieste* to the

Eventually the PX-15 will be used for salvage operations.

deepest abyss. In the face of such a dangerous experiment, most men would have made mild protestations and then quietly accepted the Navy's "disappointing" decision, but not Jacques Piccard. He continued the battle.

Finally, he pointed out a clause in his contract which allowed him the final decision on dives which might present a "special problem." The Navy was forced to agree, then, that a dive to the sea's nadir certainly posed every possibility of an unusual situation. It would be Piccard as pilot, and Walsh as observer. A deeply disappointed Rechnitzer turned to the surface problems of the mission.

On January 23, 1960, the deepest dive began. Piccard and Walsh stared at the sonic depth finder intently. A shadow showed on the graph, marking the echo of the sonic beam striking the bottom.

"There it is, Jacques," said Walsh. "We've found it!"

And for diver support. (GRUMMAN AVIATION ENGINEERING CORP. ARTIST'S CONCEPTS)

Piccard nodded, and then returned to his porthole, which was tiny inside and large outside, wedge-shaped to withstand the mighty pressure. Lights suspended from the float illuminated an area outside the sphere. Walsh counted off the final fathoms.

"32 . . . 28 . . . a nice trace now (on the depth finder) . . . 25 . . . 24 . . ." intoned Walsh.

Past the port flashed a tiny red shrimp, in itself an important discovery, for scientists had never been sure whether or not life existed at such extreme depths.

". . . 18 . . . 15 . . . 10 . . ." droned Walsh, who was watching the recorder. "You can see the bottom? Good!"

Slowly into the lights of the *Trieste* came the bottom of the deepest trench in the oceans of the world. It was firm, light-colored, with a brownish cast to it, and flat. With nearly 200,000 pounds of pressure crushing on her metal sphere (but not on her float, which had been equalized by inflowing water), the *Trieste* balanced delicately on her metal chain which had partly coiled on the bottom.

The deepest known point in the ocean had been conquered by man. But of far greater significance to the mission, directly beneath the cone of light from the *Trieste*'s forward arc lamp, lying on the bottom and apparently either dazed or hypnotized by the light, was a type of flatfish resembling a sole. It was one foot long and six inches across, a true bony teleost fish. As the light bathed it for the first time in its life (or the life of any of its ancestors), it rolled its eyes upward to examine the alien object which had entered its world, and then slowly and carefully wiggled away. Why did it have eyes in a world of total darkness since time began? This is only one of the many questions posed to scientists by the dive of the *Trieste*.

The two men in the sphere exchanged a heartfelt handshake, for they knew that oceanographers in particular would recognize the significance of this great discovery.

For twenty minutes the *Trieste* hovered at the bottom of the Challenger Deep as the occupants observed more marine life, including another red shrimp, and floor surface markings which suggested trails of living creatures.

Finally, reluctantly, Piccard tripped the ballast-release button, and iron shot poured from the containers. The *Trieste* shuddered slightly and then started upward while both men watched the bottom fade into the mist below. They were returning to the world of sunshine, light and warmth.

At almost exactly her estimated time of arrival on the surface, *Trieste*'s float and sphere began to rock gently. The rocking was surface-wave action, and told the men below that she was at the end of her journey. Support ships rushed to her as the two men crawled through the access tube and stood on the wave-washed deck. The *Trieste* waited calmly for her tenders.

Her job was finished. She had gone as deep as she could go, for there were no deeper places in the world. No more records would be set by her, for she had set the ultimate record. Her life, from that point on, would be one of exploration and a study of varying depths in the ocean. Eventually she retired, after 128 successful dives, and she is now in the Smithsonian Institution where she can be admired by all visitors.

But her builder and pilot, Jacques Piccard, was only beginning. He turned next to the designing and piloting of a strange undersea "drifting" vessel. Known as the *PX-15,* the 48-foot-long craft will submerge in Florida and drift with the Gulf Stream all the way to Canada. Since there will be no engine noise, scientists expect to learn much about the life and habits of the undersea creatures met along the way. Five men will make the strange voyage in the porthole-lined vessel at depths of from three hundred to two thousand feet and will be carried almost where the current dictates.

The pilot will be Jacques Piccard, one of the world's foremost deep-sea explorers, a scientist who is willing to back his ideas with action, regardless of the risk, as his father did before him.

Bob Manry works on the damaged hull of Tinkerbelle in the driveway of his home near Cleveland shortly after the boat was purchased.
(All photos in this chapter, except as otherwise indicated, from Tinkerbelle, by Robert Manry, Harper & Row, Publishers)

After losing his chance with the 25-foot ocean-going yacht, Manry modifies Tinkerbelle in the family garage for their voyage across the ocean. Here he is adding the tiny cabin. (COURTESY ROBERT MANRY)

Robert N. Manry

MOST OF US are ordinary people, not scientists, world-famous explorers or adventurers. We are average people, with neither the skill nor the desire to dive to the deepest depths to prove a scientific point, or to discover new things about the sea.

So we go on each day, pursuing our own work or studies, dreaming about the exploits of the ocean fighters, but no more. Most of us are normal, everyday citizens . . . but that does not necessarily mean stuffy or staid or totally set in our ways. A few of us still have the spirit of adventure. Consider, for example, Robert Neal Manry of Cleveland, Ohio.

Manry worked every day at the office of the *Cleveland Plain Dealer* as a copy editor—not the most exciting job in the world, though a pleasant, steady one by any standard. He was married, had two children, a modest but comfortable home in the Cleveland suburb of Willowick, was loved by his family, his friends and his co-workers, and considered to be a solid, dependable man in every respect.

The Manry family, living close to Lake Erie, made a normal decision for people in the upper-middle-income bracket—they decided to purchase a boat. Not a fancy cabin cruiser, but just a little sailboat in which they could have fun on the near-shore waters. It did have to be a "special" boat, to be sure, for Manry had long expressed the sincere notion that a boat should be an almost living, breathing part of a family. Naturally, the boat would have to be carefully chosen, and then respectfully treated.

Supplies are loaded aboard Tinkerbelle *at the harbor at Falmouth. Chances are the skipper of the* Island Queen *wouldn't take her across the ocean, but Manry is just about ready to leave.* (COURTESY ROBERT MANRY)

Many thousands of American families feel the same way, and make the same decision. But what Bob Manry did was most unusual, and became one of the great sagas of the sea.

They found their boat finally, for Manry saw the want ads of the *Plain Dealer* before the paper went on the streets, and so was able to get first chance at whatever he thought he might like. The final selection was a hull not much more than thirteen feet long which lay upside-down in the back yard of a private home, damaged and forlorn-looking, but which Manry felt was what he had been seeking. Something about the boat seemed to cry out, "I am not dead. I will carry you wherever you wish to go. Give me a chance!"

Manry bought the craft from the people who owned her and, as if to confirm his inner feelings, noted tears in their eyes as they watched him haul her away. Still, to be practical, the hull was in poor shape, and so for weeks

Manry worked at rebuilding it, using the garage as his workshop after consigning the family car to the street. Perhaps this was the period when man and boat came to know and respect each other. Eventually, with a rebuilt bottom and a paint job, and repairs on the tiny deck, the boat began to look presentable. She was considered a member of the Manry family as the others pitched in to help. They christened her *Tinkerbelle*.

Tinkerbelle proved to be a friendly companion on the waters of Lake Erie. She was solid, obedient, seaworthy, and responsive to the helmsman's every whim at an instant's notice.

On the high waves of Lake Erie, which ran up to eight feet at times, Manry noted *Tinkerbelle*'s smooth handling and lack of fear. She shook the water from her bow and asked for more, easily taking anything the lake could impose, much like a larger, sturdier vessel.

Robert Manry had always wanted to cross the Atlantic in a small craft. He had planned to go with a friend in a twenty-five-foot sloop. Everything was ready. Manry had obtained a leave of absence from his job, his family had agreed to the great adventure, and then the whole undertaking was cancelled. His partner, convinced by others that the voyage was foolhardy and ill-advised, withdrew both himself and his sloop.

Manry was heartbroken. Still, as he went on with his job, he began to consider. He already had the leave of absence and his family's consent. Why not simply switch a couple of minor details in the plan? Rather than in company, he could go alone, and instead of traveling in the larger sloop, he could ride in *Tinkerbelle*.

The idea seemed unthinkable, on the face of it, yet basically sound. *Tinkerbelle* had already proven her ability to withstand the elements. She was sound and tight. With certain modifications, there was no reason to assume she could not make the long journey. And so, without telling anyone but his family of the mild change of plans, Manry began to modify.

He added a small cabin to the already small boat, then made the entire craft watertight when the cabin door was closed. He turned *Tinkerbelle* into a "cork" by adding polyeurethane material in the spaces between her deck beams, and then added a heavy weight to her daggerboard-keel. He concluded he had a virtually unsinkable vessel which would ride the waves rather than resist them, and one which would return upright even if rolled onto her beam ends.

He taught himself navigation by sextant, though his first shot with the instrument from his front porch in Cleveland put his position somewhere in Canada. He kept at it, though, and soon he was able to use the sextant skillfully—at least from his porch.

Food and supplies became Manry's next order of business, and into *Tinkerbelle*'s scant storage space he packed food and water for the journey, plus spare parts and survival equipment. He fashioned a radar reflector to raise aloft on the mast when in the heavily traveled shipping lanes—one of his greatest fears was being rammed by a huge ship which couldn't even see the little boat. He packed a sail-repair kit, but decided against an outboard motor, determined to make the trip by sail or not at all.

Manry even contemplated the possibility of an attack of appendicitis while alone on the ocean and considered having his appendix removed before the trip. The chance of such an attack, however, was so remote that he finally decided to take along antibiotics instead, reasoning they would hold down any infection until he could reach help.

He stowed away several can openers to allay his mother's fear that he would find himself far at sea with no means of opening his canned food supplies. He applied for extra insurance on his own life, to protect his family in case the voyage turned into a tragic folly.

At sea with the American flag flying. (COURTESY ROBERT MANRY)

The Belgulf Glory *hove to and provided Bob Manry with a memorable meal along the way, after ascertaining that he was not a sailor in distress.* (COURTESY ROBERT MANRY)

His friends at the newspaper, still under the impression that he was going in a much larger boat, presented him with a bottle of brandy which was to serve as an emergency communications device. The instructions with the bottle directed him to "remove the contents, insert a message asking for help, then launch the bottle." Had they known the actual circumstances, they would perhaps have been less facetious, for no man had ever sailed across the stormy North Atlantic Ocean in such a tiny vessel.

Passports and vaccinations filled his final moments of preparation for he had every reason to believe that he would eventually land at a foreign shore. Finally he signed a disclaimer, relieving the Coast Guard of any responsibility for his safety, and everything seemed ready.

On June 1, 1965, at 10:30 in the morning, with a bright sun shining and sparkling off the water, Robert Manry and *Tinkerbelle* sailed out of the harbor at Falmouth, Massachusetts, and into the open sea.

WELCOME TO BRITISH WATERS! YOU ARE "BIG NEWS" AND WE SHALL BE BRINGING GENTLEMEN OF THE PRESS TO SEE YOU TOMORROW 8th AUG — AT APPROX NOON YOUR PRESENT POSITION IS :- 4945N 1220W

FROM :- Wg Cdr. R.A. CARSON O.C. N°42 SQUADRON ROYAL AIR FORCE ST. MAWGAN GOOD LUCK

Two notes dropped by airplanes from the Royal Air Force to welcome Bob Manry and Tinkerbelle *into British waters.*
(COURTESY ROBERT MANRY)

He had broken the ties which men put upon themselves, and he was finally living his great dream. Win or lose, easy or difficult, he was a happy man.

And he was a confident man. In his mind he reviewed all of the details and preparations he had made. With nothing left to chance, he had done everything possible to assure a safe and successful voyage, in spite of *Tinkerbelle*'s small size. He was sure he would reach Falmouth, England, in good shape and in good time.

He never lost confidence, though much happened in between. Perhaps a part of the sureness was love for his boat. He never referred to "his" voyage, but rather "our" voyage, and always credited his craft instead of himself, even to naming his exciting book *Tinkerbelle.*

But tall, mustached, handsome Manry is an exceptional man, and given to handing credit about when he easily could, and perhaps should, take it

70

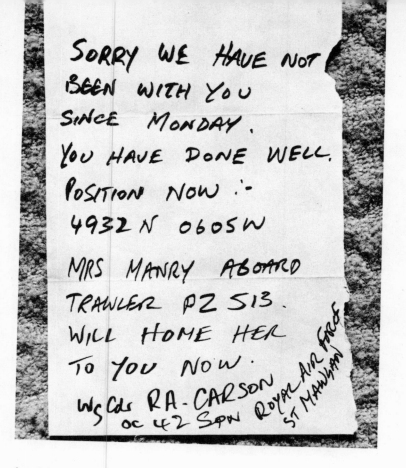

SORRY WE HAVE NOT
BEEN WITH YOU
SINCE MONDAY.
YOU HAVE DONE WELL.
POSITION NOW :-
4932 N 0605W

MRS MANRY ABOARD
TRAWLER PZ 513.
WILL HOME HER
TO YOU NOW.
WgCdr R.A.CARSON
OC 42 SQN ROYAL AIR FORCE
ST MAWGAN

for himself. Unknown when he left Falmouth, he maintained his modesty long after becoming an international figure.

A single-handed trip across the Atlantic is a lonely venture, particularly since lone sailors always attempt to steer clear of the shipping lanes to reduce the chance of a collision at sea. But Manry did not find the voyage lonely; in fact, on occasion, he found the sea quite crowded.

He had fallen into a deep sleep in the cramped cabin of *Tinkerbelle* after one week at sea. The week had been one of losing and regaining courses, storms which tossed the little craft about like a cork, hallucinations about a hitchhiker (these images bothered him throughout the voyage), and seeing many other ships. In all, he had dropped into a near-coma from sheer exhaustion, confident that *Tinkerbelle* would remain upright and afloat, and that the masthead light would warn off any approaching ships.

Then voices of men worked their way into his consciousness. In his

Manry's wife helps with answers after being brought out to welcome Bob off England.
(COURTESY ROBERT MANRY)

stupor he nevertheless realized that he was far at sea and alone except for his nightmares.

AAAAHHHOOOOOOOOOOGA! AAAAHHHOOOOOOOOOOGA!

The klaxon blasts came howling directly over the tiny cabin and shattered Manry's sleep. Instantly aware, he could almost feel the sharp bow of a ship slicing through the hull of the *Tinkerbelle*. He bounded erect and dashed out of the cabin, almost over the side, but in a final instant, he saw the huge black side of a submarine which had pulled quietly alongside, close enough to reach out and touch.

The men looking down from the bridge of the sub (the U.S.S. *Tench*) were confident that they had found a drifting dinghy, and then, when Manry came

A part of the welcoming crowd and fleet at Custom House quay, which met Manry on his arrival in England. Tinkerbelle *is circled.* (COURTESY LONDON DAILY MIRROR)

forth, a sailor in distress. They offered assistance. As calmly as possible, for his heart was still beating wildly, Manry declined, explaining that he was sailing his boat across the ocean. The men on the submarine nodded sagely, with side glances at each other, and finally moved off to submerge.

By the fourteenth day, during a wild storm, the exhausted Manry was once again torn by nightmarish hallucinations. This time he found himself in a place of sea mountains, with a strange gnome by the name of MacGregor. Others were present during this hallucination (which lasted several hours), including Manry's son Robin, who was in desperate trouble at a place called Ada's Landing. During his fight to get to Ada's, Manry was swept overboard four times, though he was mentally unable to comprehend the deadly danger he was in. He finally sailed in a new direction under the orders of a dwarf by the name of Gunga Din and found the steps leading to the sea mountains. Nearby was Ada's Landing, he was assured, but he decided (to his great good fortune) to sleep a bit before proceeding. When Manry awoke, his companions were gone and the hallucination was over.

Two more times Manry was knocked overboard by violent storms, but each time he had his lifeline tied tightly around his waist. As the strange voyage proceeded, he met ship after ship, each one offering assistance to what they imagined was a shipwrecked sailor. Considering the circumstances, this was an understandable reaction. One ship's captain, from the 18,000-ton *Belgulf Glory,* insisted that Manry accept a fresh-cooked meal from his galley. It became the most memorable meal of the entire voyage.

On August 6, an airplane from the Royal Air Force swooped low over *Tinkerbelle,* and for the first time Manry realized that he had become a celebrity. At that point, however, he had no inkling of the fame awaiting him at the conclusion of his harrowing voyage. The plane dropped canisters of fruit and a message which gave Manry a welcome to British waters, as well as informing him that his voyage had become worldwide news.

And if he thought the ocean had been "crowded" before, the situation now became even more so. The last few days of the voyage brought a crowd of newsmen competing for the privilege of interviewing him at sea, while sightseeing vessels and aircraft buzzed around and overhead.

On August 15, Manry sighted his first landfall, Bishop's Rock Light, on the coast of England, and two days later, after fighting delaying currents and winds, he sailed into the harbor at Falmouth, England. He accepted a tow at the last moment to get through hundreds of small boats which had

74

come out to meet him and also to assure his arrival during daylight, so the celebration of the townspeople would not be delayed.

Bobbing along behind a cutter, *Tinkerbelle* was almost lost in a sea of sails as the flotilla crowded in for a close look at the intrepid seaman who had sailed a "chip" across one of the most turbulent oceans in the world, the formidable North Atlantic. Manry waved and smiled, anticipating the meeting ashore with his family, who had been flown to England by the *Cleveland Plain Dealer* to await his arrival.

What did the voyage of *Tinkerbelle* and Bob Manry prove in the grand scheme of things? Scientifically, perhaps little, but then, it wasn't supposed to prove anything that way. In this day and age, when people are seemingly all tied up in strings, red tape and responsibilities, and almost afraid to try anything new, the voyage proved that the spirit of adventure in man is not dead.

The pioneering spirit which settled our country still lives deep within certain dynamic men.

Put Robert Neal Manry's name high on the list.

Dr. Andreas B. Rechnitzer (COURTESY NORTH AMERICAN ROCKWELL CORP.)

Andreas B. Rechnitzer

EXPLORING DEEP TRENCHES in the ocean floor in a submersible vessel is often dismissed airily by the scientists who do this work. The findings are the important result of the effort, while the trip to and from the area of exploration is of minor consequence. The fact that the vessel may take hours to get to the bottom, and must withstand many tons of pressure while there, seems to be of secondary importance.

That the scientific observer is often squeezed into a space about the size of a kitchen refrigerator (with at least one other man who serves as pilot) and must accomplish his studies by peering through a one-inch port-hole, is also of minor importance. Without exception, these oceanographers seem to discount the danger and discomfort of deep dives, and only become enthusiastic about the marine life and bottom conditions they have seen.

Yet, accidents do happen. And when any type of unforeseen event occurs at depths of thousands of feet, human life can be in jeopardy. Men at this depth are far beyond their own element, and quite beyond the reach of any rescue effort.

Dr. Andreas B. Rechnitzer, dynamic head of the Ocean Sciences Division of North American Rockwell Corporation and perhaps America's leading ocean research man, did confess to moments of concern during certain deep-diving research efforts. Once, in the bathyscaph *Trieste,* an event occurred which he recalls vividly.

Rechnitzer, scientist-in-charge of the Navy's Project Nekton, resulting in the deepest dive in history, stands in the conning tower of the bathyscaph Trieste. (U.S. NAVY PHOTO)

The dive was just beyond the south slope of the Isle of Capri. The *Trieste* was sliding down the nearly clifflike slope of the island as Rechnitzer watched intently through the viewing port. Deeper drifted the craft, slowly but steadily downward, through the blackness. The arc lamps illuminated a conical area outside, and Rechnitzer saw various forms of marine life moving sluggishly through the light, or along the sharply sloping bottom to one side. He watched enthralled.

Suddenly, without any warning, the *Trieste* slammed into an underwater outcropping and tilted violently. The nose of the buoyant float overhead dipped sharply downward and into the soft bottom. Inside, the two men braced themselves as the vessel rocked wildly back and forth.

But then the *Trieste* steadied herself, and all seemed well.

Checking all systems, the two men discovered a malfunction which could have proven fatal. The *Trieste* descends as the weight of extra water flowing into the float overhead is added to the weight of the ballast—iron shot pellets—contained in two "tubs" fore and aft. To bring the vessel up,

Rechnitzer and Lt. Don Walsh, on the deck of Trieste. *Although scheduled for the deepest dive, Rechnitzer was ordered to stand down at the last moment so that Jacques Piccard could make the dive. Walsh accompanied Piccard.* (U.S. NAVY PHOTO)

the pilot re-establishes buoyancy by releasing a stream of the heavy pellets.

Only one thing can defeat the system, and did off the south slope of Capri. When the nose of the *Trieste* pitched downward, the shot tube of the forward tub was jammed full of bottom mud, which almost cemented the nozzle. Although the men inside could see the nozzle through the viewing port, it might as well have been a million miles away, for there was no possible way for them to reach it.

Slowly the *Trieste* continued her downward trip.

Working calmly but quickly, the men inside cut the holding power of the electro-magnets on the aft tub, and watched a black stream of iron shot fall down through the cone of light and into the abyss far below. For several moments the shot streamed out, and still the *Trieste* sank. Then, gradually, almost imperceptibly, her descent slowed and stopped. She was dead in the water. Most of the ballast had already been dropped. The rest streamed out in a black cloud. Then there was no more.

They waited, watching their instruments and the sea outside. Finally

79

Home base for Rechnitzer and any oceanographer's dream. This is headquarters for Ocean Systems Division of North American Rockwell Corp.

(COURTESY NORTH AMERICAN ROCKWELL CORP.)

Rechnitzer saw, even before the instruments reacted, that the snowlike plankton outside the port were inching downward across the Plexiglas. The *Trieste* was finally moving up in the water. Negative buoyancy had just barely been overcome, and the vessel was slightly positive.

It was a long, long trip up, but finally they reached the sparkling surface.

Still, Rechnitzer and the others who use these deep submersibles seem to have a complete faith in their vessels, in spite of their total helplessness if anything should go amiss. On another occasion Rechnitzer rode the *Trieste* to a depth of seven thousand feet to study bottom conditions. Looking out through the tiny porthole, Rechnitzer noted a strange cylindrical object wedged into the ooze only fifteen feet away. It was an unexploded five-inch shell. If the *Trieste* had landed upon it, it might very well have exploded, destroying the craft. Needless to say, the *Trieste* was maneuvered carefully out of that area.

Under construction is this underwater habitation. Note ichthyology lab at right, diver lockout facilities at left, and Beaver Mark IV docking section at bottom. Rechnitzer is in charge of this program. (COURTESY NORTH AMERICAN ROCKWELL CORP.)

Rechnitzer was in the *Trieste* when the sphere nearly parted. The pressure of the water on the three sections of the sphere caused the epoxy glue which held them together to fail. The sections twisted apart with a loud explosion. Of course, the men inside knew, since they were still alive, that the very same pressure which had affected the glue was still holding the three sections together in a watertight seal. But what would happen when the vessel approached the surface, as it would eventually have to do? Would the three sections (a center ring and two end caps) fall apart as the pressure was reduced, and if so, at what depth would this occur? Again fortunately, the cement which had failed held sufficiently to bind the sphere together at the surface. In a prompt dry-dock operation, circular bands of steel were added to the *Trieste*.

So it is with these deep-ocean scientists. No matter how they may make light of the dangers of their work, mortal dangers are still lurking on every dive.

Andreas B. Rechnitzer does not, upon first glance, appear to be the venturesome, deep-diving scientist he is. Rather, his appearance, with an open, smiling face and a slightly balding head, might indicate a corporation lawyer. He seems to enjoy talking to people, and indeed he spends much of his time lecturing to interested groups. You might think that these deep-ocean scientists would be reserved and a bit uncommunicative, but Rechnitzer is talkative, optimistic, and ever ready to discuss the great advancements in his field. And he is prone to belittle his own accomplishments in the field, even though by now they are well known.

He gladly takes credit, however, for a rule which every man who has ever enjoyed the sport of diving will recognize: Rechnitzer is responsible for the "buddy diving" rule.

Working with Conrad Limbaugh, who later drowned in a French underground river, the two men outlined the basic rules for safety in diving. Rechnitzer's rule states that no man will dive under the surface without another diver standing by to help in any emergency. The rule has saved countless lives, including the lives of some of the men in this book. Rechnitzer is proud of the good his rule has done since those early diving days. It was much later that Limbaugh drowned—ironically, while diving alone.

Rechnitzer's "most exciting moments" in a career of adventure are typical of the scientific mind. Was it the time in the *Trieste* when, at a depth of 19,000 feet in the Mariana Trench, every circuit blew out in a blinding flash of light and the vessel stood dead in the depths, smoke filling the sphere?

No, though Rechnitzer admits to a quickening of the pulse. In this instance, he and Lieutenant Larry Schumaker, who was with him, merely studied the problem, located the difficulty, and corrected it.

"After all," he said, "there was nobody else we could call on for help."

Was it the time when he was diving with Conrad Limbaugh and his jury-rigged, homemade equipment failed at 140 feet? No, for he merely made a controlled free ascent, and though gasping for air at the surface and nearly fainting, he was safe.

Was it the time when he ruptured blood vessels in his throat while returning from a scuba dive of 140 feet, and reached the surface unable to breathe due to the blood and froth in his mouth? No, for though he was frightened, suspecting that his lungs had ruptured, he had done as he had been trained to do, and he was, after a rest, safe and had only minor injuries.

This is a part of the Rechnitzer program to develop diver transport vehicles which will carry divers to and from underwater work. Here engineers are testing an SDV (swimmer delivery vehicle) simulator in a company tank at Ocean Systems Division.

(COURTESY NORTH AMERICAN ROCKWELL CORP.)

Was it the time when he was diving with astronaut Scott Carpenter on a photographic mission, and in the four-knot current they realized they were drifting far from the safety of the diving boat? Rechnitzer could not drop the camera and swim for the boat, which was by then only a dot on the horizon, for the camera was worth more than $4,000. And burdened with heavy gear, neither man could make headway in the strong currents. Calmly analyzing the situation, Rechnitzer aimed his camera at the disappearing boat and flashed the strobe unit repeatedly until he had attracted attention.

Rechnitzer's most exciting moments were none of these things. They were, rather, (1) the time he discovered a sacrificial well once used by the Mayas, (2) the time he discovered a sunken ship dating back to the time of Columbus, and (3) the time he shot the rapids of the Colorado River (with Scott Carpenter and automobile-builder and racer Carroll Shelby). These were missions of discovery, and discovery is what most stirs the mind of a true scientist.

Andreas Rechnitzer was the scientific chief of Project Nekton, the Navy effort to reach the deepest point of the ocean with the *Trieste*. He was scheduled to make the final, deepest dive, and at the last moment was ordered to stand aside in deference to Jacques Piccard. It was a bitter disappointment for Rechnitzer, though he is still credited with the success of the hazardous dive. He was called to the White House shortly thereafter and presented with the Navy's Distinguished Civilian Service Award by President Dwight D. Eisenhower. Not bad, he recalls with a chuckle, for a man who did not wear shoes until he was thirteen years old.

Rechnitzer's original B.S. degree was earned at Michigan State University in 1947, and his M.A. at the University of California in 1951. Then he acquired his Ph.D. in 1956 at the college which every young potential oceanographer dreams of, Scripps Institution of Oceanography at La Jolla, California.

All of the work of this famous oceanographer is not deep underwater. An ancient Spanish caravel he located was found in relatively shallow water while he was leading the 1965 CEDAM Quintana Roo Expedition in Yucatan. Hundreds of artifacts were brought up from the decaying hulk, including two greatly prized bronze cannons. On the same expedition Rechnitzer found many Indian artifacts dating back 8,500 years.

Rechnitzer is one of the young men representing the new breed of ocean experts. These men were in school when Cousteau and his followers were learning the first facts about underwater exploration and conquest. The new explorers now combine their rigid training with modern equipment to forge

84

Diver's energy will be conserved for actual work by the use of these SDV's, as shown in this artist's concept. (COURTESY NORTH AMERICAN ROCKWELL CORP.)

ahead much faster. They learn more about the ocean, and they learn it more quickly, thanks to the men who went before them and the equipment they developed.

And a still newer breed will come along, for today young people are considering the field of oceanography as a career. Some experts are now predicting that as much time and money will be devoted to ocean studies as to space studies. Does Rechnitzer feel that the adventure is gone?

"No!" he says emphatically. According to Andreas Rechnitzer, only the bare surface of this science has been scratched. Great adventures and discoveries to satisfy the most scientific mind still await the young oceanographer now considering the field.

Today Rechnitzer directs a division of North American which conducts both basic and applied research in the ocean sciences. These cover biological,

Artist's concept shows Rechnitzer's Beaver Mark IV manned submersible performing photo documentation of a new undersea oil wellhead. One of the device's divers has locked-out and is preparing to install a tank of breathing gas in the rack of the adjacent habitat, where oil drillers are living. (COURTESY NORTH AMERICAN ROCKWELL CORP.)

physical, chemical and geological oceanography. Research in habitation under the sea is an important phase of Rechnitzer's Ocean Systems Division. Advanced geometric shapes for increased underwater performance are also under study. An underwater research and test station which will serve initially as a means for close observation and support of divers, manned submersibles, habitats and other equipment, and eventually as a part of the division's sea-colonization research program, is being developed. Also under construction is the division's research vessel, the *Beaver MK IV*. This submersible will have diver lock-out facilities from which a diver may leave and re-enter the vessel when she is in shallower water. More than a research craft, she will also serve as a rescue device. She will be able to dive to two thousand feet, and will have remote-contról manipulators so that the men inside can use tools for maintenance, salvage, or construction, and pick up marine samples.

This is the work of the modern oceanographer, and Dr. Andreas B. Rechnitzer is most representative of this new scientist—white-frocked in a laboratory, rubber-suited in diving gear, and sweating it out in a cabin at depths of many thousands of feet.

Engineer prepares a model of Rechnitzer's Beaver Mark IV for wind tunnel testing to determine hydrodynamic characteristics. (COURTESY NORTH AMERICAN ROCKWELL CORP.)

Sir Francis Chichester. (WIDE WORLD PHOTO)

Francis Chichester

A STORM AT SEA is a terrifying example of nature at her worst. Waves rise in giant walls of water, crashing into whirling maelstroms of destruction, the wind screams, the sky is black and menacing with its quick-moving clouds, and the turbulent water all around is cold and dark—and waiting.

On record are waves over one hundred feet high, rolling along for hundreds of miles in the open ocean, demolishing everything in their path.

Perhaps almost as terrifying as a storm is the total, desolate loneliness of an ocean becalmed, or an absence of human companionship for hundreds, and perhaps thousands, of miles.

Yet even with such deterrents as storm, calm and loneliness, some intrepid men have battled the sea on its own terms by sailing across it alone, often in a boat designed only for smaller bodies of water or for much less ambitious cruises.

One man—dubbed the "Ancient Mariner" due to his relatively advanced age—is perhaps the dean of all small-boat, long-distance, lone sailors. He decided to sail his small vessel across every ocean, around the world! Because of the great hazards of his venture, he was knighted by the Queen of England when only halfway around.

It is not known why men attempt such missions. Perhaps they do it because they are driven by something inside them, or perhaps merely because, like the summit of a mountain, the ocean "is there." It cannot be for monetary rewards, for most adventurers acquire little or nothing from such a successful

At age 63, Chichester prepares to sail Gipsy Moth III *in the race for the Observer Trophy across the Atlantic.* (WIDE WORLD PHOTO)

voyage. They may write a book, or sell their story to a magazine, but, in most cases, the money does not nearly compensate for the risk taken. Men sometimes sail away in a small craft, and occasionally the battered wreck of their boat, or pieces of it, are found later by a passing ship. More often, though, nothing at all is ever found again.

Men continue to challenge the sea in this dangerous manner, and a few have attempted to explain why. John W. Goetzcke, who sailed for America from Singapore in a thirty-one-foot yacht, merely enjoyed being alone, without "man, woman, child or whatever" for company. He did not reach his destination. Kenneth Weis of Canada made a solo eight thousand-mile trip to New Zealand in a twenty-foot boat because he felt he had to "get out of the rat race." Robert Manry sailed across the Atlantic Ocean in a tiny boat because he had always wanted to sail across the Atlantic Ocean in a tiny boat.

David Johnstone and John Hoare, two Englishmen, decided to row across the Atlantic Ocean. Later, their boat was found drifting six hundred miles south of Newfoundland, abandoned. In a sealed locker aboard was their log, with the final entry reading, "No rowing today because of north-northeast winds, eight to ten miles per hour." The next day a hurricane had smashed out of the north-northeast. Johnstone and Hoare were never heard from again.

But Chichester, the Ancient Mariner, was heard from. Word of his epic voyage, as it progressed, was flashed around the world, day by day. He became a legend in the timeless story of men against the sea. What many people did not know as they read, fascinated, of Chichester's progress was that his entire life was a legend.

The same Francis Chichester, at twenty-eight years of age and only three months after first learning to fly, made a solo flight from England to Australia, the second such flight in the history of aviation to that time. As a young man, the pattern was already developing.

Francis Chichester was born the son of a rural parson, but he was not an average child by any means. His rebellion started while attending the Marlborough School in England. At seventeen, he abandoned any plan to go to Oxford or Cambridge, and instead moved to New Zealand, where he worked at mining, door-to-door selling, and gold prospecting. His vigorous initiative manifested itself when he made a modest fortune in real estate. Then his interest in aviation began. He returned to England, learned to fly, and made his solo flight back to Australia.

To a man like Chichester, this would naturally lead to a longer, more complex flight—perhaps around the world. He tried, but this trip ended against some telephone lines in Japan and Chichester was seriously injured. He returned to England and taught navigation in the Royal Air Force during World War II. Afterwards, he formed his own map and chart company.

Turning to the sea at an age when many men are giving up strenuous activities, Chichester sailed across the Atlantic Ocean six times. He established a thirty-three-day record for such a voyage in 1952. He was by then fifty-one years old and was supposedly dying of cancer.

At the age of fifty-seven he was advised by physicians to have a lung removed, but his wife had a premonition that the operation would be fatal, so he ignored the doctors and turned once again to the sea. Frail and wan-looking, he entered still another transatlantic sailing race, and though few sportsmen imagined he would even live to cross the finish line, he won the event easily.

And so, in 1966, having already lived a life which read like a story book, Francis Chichester prepared to embark upon his most astonishing voyage.

The peppery sixty-five-year-old man announced that he would sail around the world. Of course, he would sail alone. His boat would be the now famous *Gipsy Moth IV*.

Built as an ocean-going racer for a crew of six, *Gipsy Moth* was extensively refitted so that one man could sail her. She drew seven feet and had only 854 square feet of sail in spite of her total displacement of 23,000 pounds. The largest sail was 289 square feet. Below decks the ship was divided into three main sections: forward, the storage compartment into which Chichester loaded most of his food and drink; amidships, the saloon section, or lounge, with two berths; and aft, just forward of the cockpit, the galley, cooking and eating area, and skipper's berth.

One of the most unusual features Chichester designed for the *Gipsy Moth* was an elaborate self-steering system, a system of lines linked to the rudder of the ship, that would keep the *Gipsy Moth* on course even while the skipper slept. If the ship should veer off course, an alarm system sounded immediately. Chichester also installed a radio direction finder, an echo-sounding depth gauge, and a speed gauge, plus a mechanical log to measure the distance traveled.

So, on August 27, 1966, Francis Chichester set sail from Plymouth, England. Many people, understandably, thought him mad. Aboard the *Gipsy Moth* was six hundred pounds of stores in two chief categories, fruits and vegetables (Chichester is a vegetarian), and alcoholic beverages. The *Gipsy Moth* sailed southwest, and disappeared over the horizon. Win or lose, succeed or fail, he was on his way.

"The only way to live to the full is to do something which depends on physical action, on the senses, and at the same time on the man-developed parts of the brain," radioed Chichester. He was doing that, living to the full.

But for how long? Could he navigate and handle the saucy *Gipsy Moth* throughout the hazardous days and weeks ahead?

On September 16, he was off the coast of Africa, sailing almost due south toward the Cape of Good Hope. All was well with both sailor and vessel, but loneliness was a poignant problem. He sank into moods of depression, unable to play musical recordings stowed aboard by his son, for they reminded him too strongly of home and family.

He suffered pain from some minor injuries. Once he broke off a tooth—but this wiry man of the sea merely filed the tooth down with a steel rasp.

On October 3 he turned east and approached the Cape of Good Hope. By October 27 he was well past it and into the vast Indian Ocean. Passing

92

ships and planes reported on his progress, and from time to time Chichester radioed his position. All was well with the Ancient Mariner.

On November 13 he was deep into the Indian Ocean, thousands of miles from any shore, halfway between Africa and Australia, but a month later, on December 12, 1966, he reached Sydney, Australia, his "halfway point." A tumultuous welcome greeted him, one which he felt was far more than he deserved. He was "only doing what he wanted to do." Besides, he hadn't done it all, yet.

Since he had already accomplished an amazing feat of skill and endurance by sailing *Gipsy Moth IV* to Australia, his friends tried to persuade him to forget the remainder of the voyage. The worst, they knew, was yet to come. Ahead of the sleek little sailboat would be the formidable Cape Horn, at the southern tip of South America, where hundreds of ocean-going ships had perished. Ahead, too, would be the vast and infinitely lonely South Pacific.

Chichester checks his radar reflector which will warn oncoming ships of his presence during his lonely voyage. (WIDE WORLD PHOTO)

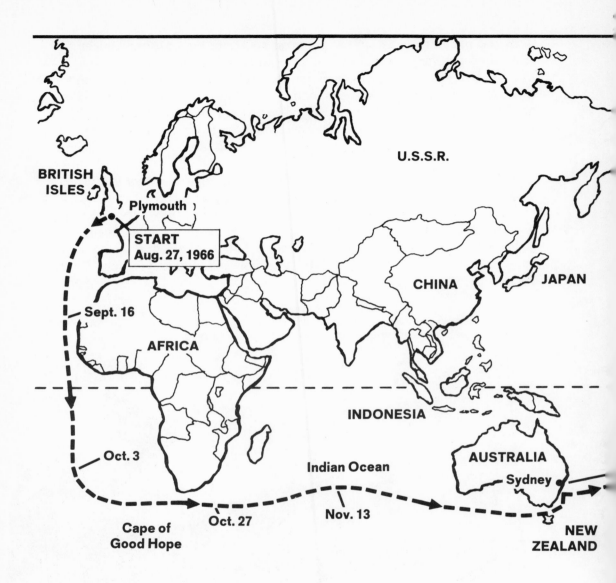

Route of Sir Francis Chichester and Gipsy Moth IV, *with dates.*

Chichester—Sir Francis now—would not be dissuaded from his dream, and so, on January 29, 1967, he sailed out of Sydney Harbor, heading east

94

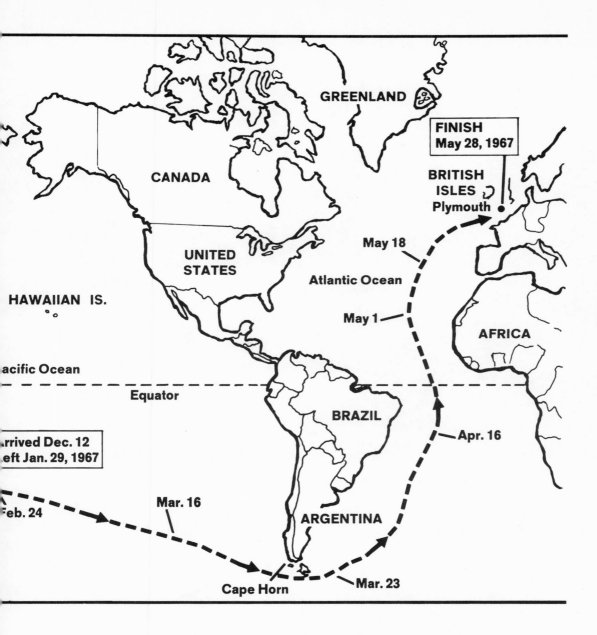

GREENLAND

FINISH
May 28, 1967

BRITISH
ISLES
Plymouth

CANADA

UNITED
STATES

May 18

Atlantic Ocean

HAWAIIAN IS.

May 1

AFRICA

acific Ocean

Equator

BRAZIL

Arrived Dec. 12
Left Jan. 29, 1967

Apr. 16

Feb. 24

Mar. 16

ARGENTINA

Cape Horn

Mar. 23

for South America. The next time he stepped ashore, if he did step ashore
again, would be in England at the end of his voyage. And so, for a time, he

Gipsy Moth IV rolls in the heavy seas off Cape Horn during Chichester's long voyage around the world. (WIDE WORLD PHOTO)

disappeared from sight. Notes from his log, however, give an insight to his experiences:

"Something that reminds you that you are a human being like everyone else is unbearably sad."

Approaching Cape Horn, he felt that he was at the "heel of hell."

Passing Cape Horn, he noted, "My overwhelming impression of the past week is one of fear . . . I had a feeling of helplessness."

His weight dropped. He felt sad and terribly lonely. The voyage was telling on his health, yet he sailed on. Occasionally a ship or airplane would

96

sight him. The world became interested once again in the fantastic voyage of the lone mariner, then excited, and finally, as Sir Francis Chichester sailed up the Atlantic Ocean, inflamed.

Though the voyage had seemed impossible from the start, and particularly so for an elderly, ill man, it suddenly seemed apparent that Chichester was going to make it. He was nearing England and home. On May 1, he was once again far off the coast of Africa, and with favorable winds well north of that point by May 18. Chichester could sense his goal ahead in the mists.

Gala welcoming plans were arranged. Plymouth, a normally peaceful city of 250,000, grew to twice that size as spectators and newsmen poured into the area. Thousands of boats crisscrossed the harbor, awaiting the arrival of the *Gipsy Moth*. First a speck on the horizon, she grew larger, and boats of every size and shape rushed out to meet her.

On May 28, 1967, Sir Francis Chichester stepped ashore. Great honors followed. When Queen Elizabeth II formally confirmed his knighthood, she used the same sword which had been used to knight Sir Francis Drake.

Tired and gaunt, but happy and appearing in good health, Francis Chichester finally escaped the crowds and relaxed with his wife and son. He had been at sea, alone, for 266 days. The time had come for a peaceful retirement.

Surely Chichester would agree to this, especially after completing his greatest sail. So he did vow that he would seek no further adventure . . . "not for a week."

Already this outstanding seaman and skilled navigator is planning another solo trip around the world. Of course, having done it once, it could become routine. And so, to remove this dull possibility, he is charting a more challenging, more dangerous route.

Captain John Ridgway (left) and Sergeant Chay Blyth (center) listen attentively as fisherman Bill Stephens advises them about oarlocks on their ocean-crossing dory English Rose III. (WIDE WORLD PHOTO)

John Ridgway and Chay Blyth

CAPTAIN JOHN RIDGWAY is a paratrooper in the British Army, a solidly built, stony-eyed fighting man, accustomed to rugged competition. All his life he has competed with his fellow man—in the boxing ring, in the paratroopers, and finally in rowing matches, a grueling sport. According to his own definition, he is a "physical-experience seeker."

Sergeant Chay Blyth is a paratrooper in the British Army who, when he was a private, served in the platoon of the then Second Lieutenant Ridgway. A stolid Scot, he is perhaps even more rugged than Ridgway. Nothing bothers him, on the surface at least. He faces a situation, decides upon the best course of action to follow, and follows it.

At 5:30 P.M. on June 4, 1966, these two courageous men went through the inlet at Orleans on Cape Cod and headed out to sea on a voyage home. Their boat, a dory; their motive power, oars.

Their plan? To row across the treacherous North Atlantic Ocean, from the United States to England.

Such a feat had been accomplished only once before. In 1896, Frank Samuelson and George Harbo had done it. As if to add a pinch of competitive spice, another team, British journalist David Johnstone and public relations man John Hoare, had set out on the same voyage less than two weeks earlier. As Ridgway and Blyth rowed out into the ocean, they did not know that Johnstone and Hoare would never be heard from again.

They only hoped that their carefully laid plans would bring success, and that, with great luck, they would beat the other two to the shores of England. Many small boats escorted them for the first few miles at sea, but one by one they turned around and returned to shore. Soon the two men were alone on the vast ocean, dipping and pulling their oars. The truth expressed upon a small brass plaque one of the Cape Cod fishermen had affixed to the forward watertight compartment of the dory *English Rose III* became all too evident:

"O God, thy sea is so great, and my boat so small."

Now they were a mere speck on the lonely ocean, wondering why they had attempted such a journey. The possibility had first occurred to both men during a long-distance canoe race in 1960. In the dark, in the winter, on the cold waters of the river Thames in England, they became aware that they worked well as a team. Despite a turnover at a whirlpool and a resultant loss of more than a half-hour, they were able to win the seventy-mile race. Then their careers in the service separated them and it was 1965 before the venture suggested itself again. Ridgway had learned that David Johnstone was planning to row across the Atlantic. His first thought was to volunteer to join him, but he was unable to work his way through the list of the other volunteers. Finally, John Hoare was picked. Meanwhile, Ridgway became convinced that he too could row across the ocean with a qualified teammate. He wanted Blyth, and Blyth volunteered.

Still, an ocean row is not a venture in which one buys a rowboat and then, on a fine Sunday morning, sets off on the journey. Detailed planning had to follow. The Army granted them a leave of absence without pay, and the project moved forward.

Since nobody seemed willing to sponsor what Ridgway himself termed "two suicides," the team scraped together $600 themselves and purchased an open, twenty-foot dory-type boat, and they named it the *English Rose III*. Then they turned their craft over to the crusty fishermen of Cape Cod, who had had generations of practical experience in dories. For weeks they worked and practiced and modified. They added freeboard and removed keel, added a rudder and removed oarlocks, adding this and changing that. The Cape Codders worked out a system of harnesses hitched to twenty-foot safety lines so that the men would not be swept away in a storm, nor be trapped beneath the overturned boat. They mounted a compass, added four emergency radios, foul-weather clothing, rations and water. In almost every case, the two paratroopers followed the advice of the expert fishermen.

Finally, they were ready, and so they rowed away. Almost immediately

Leaving the United States, Ridgway and Blyth (nearest boat) pull out of Orleans and head for England. (WIDE WORLD PHOTO)

they were engulfed by a violent North Atlantic storm. The wind howled as the tiny craft, held only by a sea anchor, slid up and down tremendous waves. The two men huddled beneath a canvas canopy in an attempt to stay relatively dry. It was an inauspicious beginning, for they had hardly had a chance to row. Driving the dory north, the wind continued for a full day until it finally abated.

Ridgway immediately took a positional fix with his sextant in order to determine how far off course the storm had blown them. He stared in astonishment at his charts. They *couldn't* have been pushed *that* far, for his calculation placed them in the middle of the state of Vermont! Off course they were, but not in Vermont. Ridgway then discovered that the sextant had been moderately damaged during the storm.

After only five days at sea, they reached the lowest point of the entire trip. In his own thoughts, each man was discouraged and disheartened, for storms and foul weather had continued to drive them off their course. Their calculations placed them only a hundred miles off the coast of Maine, lagging far behind where they had hoped to be by then. Adding to the dilemma of their poor position, the radio announced the imminent arrival of Hurricane Alma. Everything seemed lost.

They were tired, wet, dismayed and hungry, and they had to prepare for a hurricane. Ridgway and Blyth, however, are not men given to ordinary fears or discouragements. They prepared for Alma as best they could, lashing everything down tightly, and then they slept.

Alma's screaming winds and pounding waves awakened them, but the violent storm was by then dying. Her waves were only twenty to thirty feet high, and the dory was built to withstand such waters—and more. *Rosie* climbed and dived, sideslipping down the huge mounds of water, as the two men, taking heart, held on. The storm finally moved off, and they were still alive and still afloat.

Their spirits soared momentarily. They *could* defeat the ocean! With renewed vigor, they turned *Rosie* toward the Gulf Stream and rowed. The Gulf Stream, that great meandering current of warmer water flowing up the coast of the United States and then eastward to England, was their first destination. If they could reach it, they knew that the currents from that point on would be favorable and would actually help to carry them to England. *Rosie* would go on and eventually reach English waters by herself, even with a dead crew aboard. Strongly they rowed eastward, watching for signs of the Stream.

On June 15, after a morning of rugged but, they were sure, rewarding, rowing, they encountered the trawler *Winchester,* whose skipper called out some disconcerting news. Their position was exactly 180 miles out of Boston, far from where they had planned to be after twelve days on the ocean and far from the Gulf Stream.

The logical move seemed to be to give up, board the *Winchester,* as the skipper suggested, and head back to the Massachusetts shore. They had tried, they had given it a good solid effort, and they were failing. Each man studied the other as this simple solution presented itself, and they knew the answer instinctively. To the astonishment of the skipper and crew of the *Winchester,* they refused aid and rowed away.

On June 17, they crossed over the continental shelf, which is marked by a change in the wave pattern on the surface to longer, deeper swells, and entered the true "deep" sea. Huge whales, basking in the sunlight at the surface, drifted over to examine them before sounding. Once, on a dark night in a shrouding fog, a huge vessel passed within feet of them, violently rocking *Rosie,* yet neither vessel sighted the other in the white atmospheric blanket.

The Gulf Stream drew ever nearer. On June 19, the Woods Hole research vessel *Albatross IV* hove into view and, stopping for a chat, informed them they were on course and only seventy miles from the Stream. Once again their rowing efforts were redoubled, since success was almost in sight.

The hands of both Ridgway and Blyth became at first sore and then blistered, and eventually molded themselves around the oar handles. It became difficult to unclench them, and finally almost impossible, without feeling great pain. Yet the rowing itself was not as exhausting as the two men had imagined it would be, for they had prepared themselves with rigorous exercises. They talked to each other incessantly to combat the heavy loneliness that every man has noted on the broad expanse of the empty ocean. Each day, as they estimated that the Gulf Stream was nearer, their spirits improved.

Or improved, at least, until they met the Canadian fishing boat *Robertson II.* From the captain they heard the unbelievable news that, according to his calculations, they were still seventy miles from their primary goal. Easterly wind and currents were almost canceling out their efforts, and they were barely moving ahead. Then, when they stopped to sleep at night, they were losing what little they had gained as the currents carried them back toward the United States. It was, all in all, disheartening in the extreme, yet each man reached for his oars to row onward, eastward. They were beyond the point of quitting.

Almost immediately, the wind changed. It turned around gradually until it was an ideal westerly, and *Rosie* was swept toward England. In five days they covered 150 miles, and moved into the Gulf Stream.

Hurricane Alma had ruined part of their stores early in the voyage, forcing a curtailment of their rations, and so they spent long rowing hours discussing the meals they would have to celebrate their success. They even picked the restaurants—this one for a cocktail, that one for an entrée, another for the dessert. One favorite restaurant was reluctantly removed from their list, as they were afraid they would not be able to find a parking space.

Every waking hour they rowed, and with the help of the Gulf Stream moved closer to England. In the Stream they averaged about thirty eastward miles every day. Forty degrees north latitude became their next goal, and finally, on July 23, after being blown back several times by storms, they crossed this marker. But another cut in rations became necessary, for they

Ridgway, age 27, and Blyth, age 26, row up the Thames River in London after their successful row across the Atlantic Ocean. (WIDE WORLD PHOTO)

were behind schedule. The two men began to suffer from lack of food. They tired quickly and became depressed easily.

On August 5, Captain Ridgway made these notations in his log:

> *800 miles to go.*
> *30 days rations left.*
> *I have a pain in the groin, indicating a serious infection.*

Men, and particularly sailors, have often said that the darkest part of the night is just before the dawn, and for Ridgway and Blyth it was the darkest part of the night. Bone-tired, discouraged, weak from their quarter-rations, wet and miserable, and now, with illness facing them, they were truly at their darkest hour.

But the dawn did come. The medicine which they had brought and which had not been lost by the ravages of Alma, cleared up Ridgway's infection.

104

Shortly afterward, a British tanker came into view. Invited aboard by the captain, the two adventurers ate a magnificent breakfast of hot scrambled eggs. One hour later they pushed off once again for England, their stomachs full and their spirits high. They knew then that they were going to make it.

Early in the morning, on Saturday, September 3, the wind suddenly shifted from west to south, clearing away a mist which had been hovering around them. Ridgway stared intently at the horizon for long moments.

Quietly, calmly, attempting with every nerve in his body to hold his voice steady, he said to Blyth, "That's it over there."

There was what appeared to be a thin line just over the horizon.

"Are—are you sure?" asked Blyth, refusing to look.

"Yes, I'm certain."

"I'll wait till we're closer," said Blyth. "Then I'll look. Then we'll be sure."

Blyth waited for one full hour, then Ridgway persuaded him to look.

The sergeant turned slowly on his seat to look out over the bow of *Rosie,* almost afraid of what he would not see. Then a grin crossed his weather-beaten face.

"Oh, yes, that's definite," he said. The land ahead was, by then, quite obvious.

The land on the horizon was the island of Aran, off the coast of Ireland. It was home to the two men.

Nature does not give up easily, though. A storm, seemingly intent upon thwarting their voyage at the last instant, suddenly came up and drove them skimming toward the rocks of Aran. Fighting with all their remaining strength, and with the help of a lighthouse crew from Aran, they finally beached safely.

They had succeeded. They had rowed across the Atlantic. Swarms of reporters were waiting to flash the news to the world. On the dock they were told that Johnstone and Hoare had not been seen nor heard from in many weeks.

No trace was ever found of these two adventurers.

Today Ridgway and Blyth are seeking a further challenge, perhaps a sailing race across the ocean, or anything else which might offer a chance to "get the old machine going again." Meanwhile, they have a new and deeper respect for the sea. Reading the English headlines which screamed THE BOYS WHO BEAT THE ATLANTIC, they scoff.

They did not beat the Atlantic, they insist. Rather, the Atlantic decided they were giving it a "real try," and allowed them to go free.

Admiral C. B. "Swede" Momsen. (THE NATIONAL ARCHIVES)

Charles B. "Swede" Momsen

IN THE "silent service" of submarines, disaster can strike suddenly, swiftly, and with absolutely no warning. That was especially true in the early, exciting, but certainly not glamorous, days of the pigboats of the United States Navy. On these small undersea boats a man served only because he sincerely wanted to serve. A volunteer was generally called a fool. Unlike modern nuclear-powered submarines, these were unsanitary, foul-aired vessels, smelling of fuel, oil and sweat. Not even toilets were provided for the crew. Worse, pigboats were dangerous, and one had to accept with stoic calm the very real possibility that he could be trapped and drown, for escape from a pigboat was impossible.

Few officers volunteered for the silent service then, for the Navy was all battleships and heavy cruisers. Not only was the submarine service dirty and dangerous, but it could even delay a man's promotion and stall his naval career, inasmuch as no man was considered totally reliable who would request such service.

Yes, disaster could strike swiftly, and did, for the new young skipper of the submarine *O-15*. Yet, contrary to what generally happened, he overcame the mortal danger and went on to become a Vice-Admiral in the United States Navy.

The *O-15* was on a simulated combat cruise in the Caribbean Sea, gliding along underwater with everything functioning as normally as possible when she suddenly plunged bow down at full speed. Before anything could be done, she drove her bow fifty feet into the mud at the bottom of the sea. Quickly the mud closed in, locking her fast.

"Full astern!" shouted the captain. But the O-15 didn't budge.

Knowing that he and the crew would die in a very short time in the trapped submarine, the young skipper issued another command:

"Flood the forward torpedo tubes!"

The crew moved quickly to carry out the order, though they could not understand what their captain planned. What good would it do, they wondered, to add further weight to the entrapped bow?

"Fire!" came the order. Since no torpedoes had been loaded into the tubes, the "water plugs" in each tube blasted out and the boat shuddered free as the force of the water drove at the bottom.

Charles B. ("Swede")Momsen, then only a young officer on his first command, had saved the boat and the entire crew by some quick thinking. They would not be the last men he would save, for as his career in the Navy went on, he rescued many hundreds of men both personally and through inventions. And the rescues go on today, though he is now retired.

He fought the ocean in a different way throughout his exciting career, for his prime goal was to snatch back the lives of men the sea was claiming. At great risk to his own life, he did this time after time.

Yet Swede Momsen's career started with a failure. In the Naval Academy at Annapolis, in his second year of studies, he failed Spanish. Service academies are not known for pampering failing students. They are harsh and tough. Momsen, in spite of an otherwise fine record, was "flunked out" of the academy, dismissed from the life he wanted before it had really started.

Momsen looked sufficiently like the picture we all see when we think of a tough sea captain—stocky, a body hard and tough, a jutting and tenacious-looking square jaw, eyes that bore into you, backed by an iron will to match this appearance. Momsen persuaded his Minnesota Congressman to reappoint him to the Naval Academy, and this time he not only passed Spanish but graduated in the top fifteen per cent of his class.

He was commissioned an ensign in June, 1919.

For two years, until September, 1921, he served in the surface navy on the battleships *Oklahoma* and *Maryland,* but his yearning was for a career underwater. Finally his request for transfer was approved, and he reported to the submarine base at New London, Connecticut. Before his first full command, the *O-15,* he served for one year on the *O-13* in the Panama Canal Zone.

108

Another camera portrait of the inventor of the Momsen Lung. (THE NATIONAL ARCHIVES)

Finally, in 1924, Swede Momsen was given command of the *S-1,* one of the newest, sleekest, fastest submarines in the fleet. An early assignment with the new boat perhaps led him to his career of life-saving. Until then he had been a skillful submarine captain, but not more outstanding than any other competent officer.

On a dismal September day of that same year, the inbound freighter *City of Rome,* headed toward Boston, was feeling her way in a dense fog off Block Island. Suddenly, without prior warning, she struck the partially submerged conning tower of the *S-51.* The sub, with a huge hole gashed in her side, plunged through the icy waters to the bottom, 132 feet below the surface. Only an oil slick and a pathetic little marker buoy dropped by the freighter at the point of impact marked the spot. It was the duty of the *S-1,* under the command of Lieutenant Momsen, to find her sister ship.

The sunken submarine was found, but there were no survivors. None had been expected. Ironically, several decades before, a man by the name of

Robert H. Davis, of Siebe, Gorman, Ltd. had invented a submerged-escape apparatus, but it had been regarded as something less than adequate. Submarine crews knew what to expect if their boat went down. There was no real method of either getting to them or raising the sunken submarine in time to save them. You just had to be philosophical about submarine duty.

Swede Momsen transferred to the Bureau of Construction and Repair in the Submarine Safety Test Unit, and here his skills and inventive prowess came to full flower. Submarine-escape techniques and rescue equipment became an obsession with him. Carefully, systematically, using himself as a guinea pig more often than not, he began to work on devices and techniques which would enable crews to leave a sunken submarine.

He had two escape projects in mind, one a breathing bag a man could attach to himself and rise to the surface, and the other a bell-shaped steel chamber which could be lowered to the deck of a submarine and then used to carry men up. Unfortunately, neither the American public nor the U.S. Congress was much interested in Momsen's work, or in submarine safety in general. Submariners, to most people, were still just a minority group of odd men who obviously took great risks because they enjoyed doing so.

Until one morning in December, 1927. On that cold gray morning the modern *S-4* plunged to the bottom off Provincetown with forty men aboard. Some of the men were still alive, though trapped beyond help. Divers were on her decks, but there was no way to get to the men inside. The divers could only wait helplessly outside, knowing their friends were dying, and listen to the feeble last words tapped out in code on the hull.

"P-l-e-a-s-e—h-u-r-r-y . . ." and then there was no further sound. The last man had died inside the sunken *S-4*.

Finally, the American public became aroused. Forty fine men of the Navy had died merely because there was no way to get them out. They were alive, the water was not deep, and yet they had died. And Momsen was aroused, for he was sure he had the answer.

Ironically, it was the salvaged *S-4*—a constant reminder to Momsen's crew of the importance of their job—which was used for escape experiments. On February 5, 1929, they first tested a technique which, in modified form, is still used today to rescue trapped submariners. It was the testing of the "Momsen Lung," a device which has saved countless lives since then.

On that 1929 day, Charles Momsen and Chief Torpedoman Edward Kalinowski prepared to leave the submerged, reconditioned *S-4* with Momsen's device strapped to their chests. Resembling a gas mask with a rubber

110

The "Steinke Hood," the latest in a series of submarine escape devices starting with Momsen's "lung." The Steinke method allows a submariner to breathe more naturally and to keep his vision clearer. Steinke is shown on deck. (U.S. NAVY PHOTO)

bladder attached, it had two tubes. One carried air from the mouth to the bag; the other, enclosing a canister of soda lime to purify the air, carried air from the bag back to the mouth. The bag had a capacity about equal to that of the human lung.

The two men entered the submarine's "escape trunk," a compartment which could be flooded until the pressure inside equaled the pressure outside,

111

A surprise maneuver off to starboard is pointed out to Cmdr. Sidney D. B. Merrill (left) and Under Secretary of the Navy Dan Kimball (right) by Admiral C. B. Momsen (center). (THE NATIONAL ARCHIVES)

and which had a hatch leading out. When the hatch drifted open with the equalizing pressure, the men released a marker buoy with a line attached, and knots in the line to indicate decompression stops, and then they started slowly for the surface.

The experiment was a resounding success. Both men came to the surface from the "sunken" boat in fine condition. Again and again they tested the device, deeper and deeper under the surface. It never failed, even at over two hundred feet down. Finally, twenty-six men, using the Momsen Lung "escaped" in the New London test facility tank. The Navy accepted the device, and installed it for every single crewman on every submarine in the fleet.

Momsen was awarded the Distinguished Service Medal for "courageously, repeatedly and voluntarily risking his life" in the development of the lung.

Enough accomplishment for one man? Not at all, for meanwhile Momsen was perfecting his escape trunk.

It would not be used for many years, but then it would be desperately needed in one of the most famous of all the modern submarine disasters.

During the 1930's, Swede Momsen worked at a variety of tasks in the Navy, including a term as technical director for the rash of submarine motion pictures. He was also an officer on the mine-layer *Oglala,* the submarine *Canopus* and the submarine *Augusta.* He was the officer in charge of experimental diving at the Navy Yard in New York, and here he worked with gas substitutes to search for a way to conquer the dreaded bends.

The Navy had gone twelve years without a major submarine disaster when a name which was to hit every headline and burn into the mind of every newspaper reader electrified the public on the morning of May 23, 1939. A few miles from the Isle of Shoals off Portsmouth, a new submarine was making a routine dive maneuver. An engine induction valve failed to close. The engine room flooded, killing several men there. Still, thirty-three officers and men were alive, fighting to save their boat.

But to no avail. The submarine *Squalus* settled onto the bottom, 243 feet down, beyond the limit of the Momsen Lung. Part of the crew was alive, but trapped and dying.

Luckily, this was 1939, not 1919, and the submarine was quickly located. Almost immediately the rescue attempt started. Aboard the salvage ship *Falcon,* which was standing directly over the sunken *Squalus,* was the rescue bell developed by Momsen and Commander Allan McCann.

A ten-ton, double-compartment device, it was carefully lowered to the deck of the *Squalus* and attached directly over the escape hatch. Then the water in the lower compartment of the bell was blown out with compressed air. Men in the upper compartment could drop directly onto the hatch of the submarine. They quickly opened the hatch and peered into the dark, foul interior of the sub.

Grimy, but smiling, faces stared up at them.

Four trips were made to carry men from the *Squalus* to the surface in Momsen's rescue bell, and though on the very last trip a cable snarled and the men inside had some anxious moments, the entire rescue was successful. Every man still alive when the *Squalus* went down was brought to the surface safely. It was the single most dramatic lifesaving effort in the submarine service.

Henceforth, all submariners felt a little better about service in the undersea boats. Yes, disaster could still strike swiftly and with no warning, but at least there were rescue devices and techniques available, thanks to Swede Momsen and his crew.

Momsen had reached a high point in his career, a point from which he could look back upon all the things he had accomplished. But quite often men who are driven to do great deeds or to invent wonderful inventions cannot rest, even if rest is called for. Momsen had invented and then perfected, at great risk to his own life, two devices which would eventually save countless lives. Yet his career could have started *after* his successful rescue and the salvage of the *Squalus* (during which divers made 640 dives without a mishap), and it still would have been a most distinguished one.

On one occasion, during his later work on torpedo-firing mechanisms, the then Lieutenant Commander Momsen stripped off his uniform and plunged into the water to inspect a faulty torpedo. In World War II, American submarines had been firing at enemy ships with great accuracy, but the torpedoes had been merely bouncing off the sides of these ships. It was a case of no damage and an instant warning to the enemy that a sub was prowling nearby. In an effort to learn where the malfunction was occurring, Momsen and his crew fired torpedoes into cliffs.

One torpedo triggered, but it did not explode, and it was this one which Momsen swam down to inspect. At any instant it could have blown him to bits, but through this on-the-spot observation, a new firing mechanism was developed which accounted for the destruction of thousands of tons of enemy shipping.

Tired of his "desk job," Momsen then commanded an American submarine wolf pack in the Pacific Ocean during the war. Where the German wolf packs operated in a more uncoordinated scattergun fashion, Momsen directed his own submarines in highly coordinated attacks on enemy ships. More thousands of tons of shipping plunged to the bottom.

For his distinguished work with wolf packs, Captain Momsen was awarded the Navy Cross, an award second only to the Medal of Honor.

Leaving the submarine service for a time, Momsen then commanded the battleship *South Dakota* in pre-invasion operations which included attacking enemy installations in the Tokyo area. Finally, after a brief desk job in Washington with the Navy Department, Rear Admiral Momsen was given the job of repatriating millions of people from China, Manchuria, Formosa and the Pacific Islands. After the war, Momsen helped train unskilled Japanese in efforts to integrate them into a joint American-Japanese shipping organization.

Admiral Momsen finally served for three years as Assistant Chief of

Naval Operations for Undersea Warfare; then as Commander, Submarine Force, Pacific Fleet; then as Commandant of the First Naval District in Boston; then finally in his last command, as Commander of Joint Task Force Seven.

Upon retirement from a distinguished career with the Navy, Momsen was promoted to Vice-Admiral.

It is impossible to say exactly how many lives were saved by the inventions of Admiral Momsen. During the dangerous, dirty, dark days of World War II, when submarines were lost with alarming regularity, precise records were not kept. But there are many men alive today who surfaced from a destroyed submarine wearing a Momsen Lung. And there are others who returned to the surface in a Momsen-designed rescue bell. Many more are alive because of the techniques developed by Momsen in undersea warfare, and because of his work with the faulty torpedoes.

Admiral Charles B. Momsen, who as a young ensign saved the lives of every man aboard the pigboat *O-15* by firing the torpedo tubes, spent the rest of his career saving the lives of American submariners.

William Willis, on the deck of Age Unlimited, *leaves port on his longest voyage to Australia. With a brief stop in Samoa for medical treatment, Willis was successful in making the trip alone and without help.* (WIDE WORLD PHOTO)

William Willis

WHEN MEN of the sea, including ocean experts and adventure lovers, ponder the roster of daring men in small vessels who have challenged the seas of the world, the name of one man stands out as the bravest, the most reckless, the most dramatic one of them all.

This "king of the sea" is also the oldest of the adventurers, far past the age when most men are ready to sit back to enjoy the rewards of a life of work. Probably, in spite of his age, he is also the toughest of all. He once lay alone and paralyzed on the deck of his raft, suffering from a broken back until he, himself, forced motion and action again. One trip (he has made several) was cut short only when bleeding ulcers almost ended his life.

He lives to test himself against the sea, this brave man, and he has earned in full measure the title "King Neptune." Always in a small craft, always alone, he has challenged several oceans.

He is William Willis, an astounding old man of gnarled muscles, weathered skin and laughing eyes. Other wandering sailors, usually unaware of what their fellow adventurers are doing, know and watch what Willis does. In their hearts they have a special place for this man who just won't quit. When, at the completion of one particularly grueling sea voyage, he staggered ashore in Australia, his hair and beard bleached white by the sun, and calmly said, "I'm Willis of New York," he had done far more than most. Yet he goes on. He says he will be sailing around the world alone at the age of ninety.

It isn't all pure adventure, though this is primarily what he seeks. He has demonstrated, by means of a recent voyage in which there was no fresh water aboard, that man can survive drinking sea water in proper amounts. Though over a prolonged period the salt water made him feverish and depressed, and began to affect his body, it did keep him alive for a period of time previously thought impossible.

"It is my nature to try the impossible," he calmly says, ignoring the likelihood of an agonizing death alone on the vast ocean.

Born in Hamburg, Germany, Willis, at the age of fifteen, shipped as a cabin boy on a bark bound for Mexico. Returning to Hamburg, he left for good in 1909 when he came to the United States and settled in Galveston, Texas. Willis worked as a longshoreman until he had enough money to buy a small farm and to bring his mother and two younger brothers from Germany to this new home. For ten years the family farmed, and Willis worked on the docks. Then they moved to San Francisco and an easier life.

But William Willis grew restless. During the twenties, he became an itinerant farm worker, traveling from place to place, laboring or loafing when he pleased. He was more than forty years old when he finally returned to the sea, shipping from New York as an able seaman.

Between voyages, in New York in 1938, his landlady approached him tearfully one day, stating that her son, unjustly convicted of a murder in France many years earlier, had served his term of imprisonment on infamous Devil's Island and had been officially released. But on Devil's Island, there was no full release. He was still confined to the island for a life of struggle and starvation as a *libéré*.

Willis promised the woman that he, personally, would do what he could . . . and he was off on his first unlikely adventure. He shipped on a freighter to Dutch Guiana, and after months of hardship he actually rescued the son and brought him home. The son later fought valiantly for the French Army in the Second World War.

Meanwhile, Willis served several years in the Merchant Marine, drawing ever closer to the sea. An innocent messroom conversation led him to his second great adventure. Some sailors were wondering aloud how long a man could remain alive adrift on the ocean with only starvation rations, and Willis thereupon determined to learn the answer, by practice rather than theory.

In Ecuador, in 1953, he lashed seven huge balsa wood logs together into a raft, christened the vessel *Seven Little Sisters,* and then set sail for Samoa. One hundred and fifteen days later, and after 6,700 miles on the ocean, he landed in Pago Pago. During the entire voyage the outside world had heard

118

*Well beyond the age when most men have retired, Willis here sets sail from Montauk,
L. I., for the long solo journey to England in* Little One. *He was 74 years old here.*

119

only one message from him, six days out at sea, when he sent, "Going ahead, all's well."

There were other messages—emergency messages which were not received, since all was not well on numerous occasions. Willis was heartbroken for a time. He had brought along a cat and a parrot for company, and the cat killed and ate the parrot. At one time, Willis was desperately ill, and on another occasion a shark mangled his hand. He fell overboard and nearly drowned as the raft drifted away. Only a desperate swim saved him. But he made it, all the way to Pago Pago, and the whole experience exhilarated him. He had to have more.

For several years he lectured and wrote of his adventures, capturing audiences and readers with his keen wit and sharp tongue. In 1963 he headed once again for Callao, the main port of Peru. There, building a raft of the same size as before, but this time with steel pontoons, the seventy-year-old adventurer sailed away, alone as always—on a voyage to Australia!

With his own advanced age in mind, he had christened his vessel *Age Unlimited.*

One hundred and thirty days later he put into Apia, Samoa, for a refitting. His hair had turned snow-white during the voyage, attesting to a plague of endured hardships—foul weather, broken rudders, and a serious hernia which was sapping his strength and causing him to black out with pain.

But he was not through. Bidding his raft a temporary farewell, he flew to New York for a physical checkup and some hasty medical repairs, and then returned to Samoa. Not long after, he was once again sailing toward Australia on *Age Unlimited,* the wind streaming through his white hair and beard.

His hernia recurred, and once when a block gave way and slammed him back into a mast, his lower spine was cracked. Willis was paralyzed from this injury for a week, lying helpless on the deck where he had fallen. Yet, when a British freighter approached him with an offer of help, Willis struggled to his feet and answered, "Radio my position." That was all. The tough old man couldn't quit, in spite of the odds.

After a total of 420 days on the ocean, he came ashore at Tully, a brawling seaport town on the northeast tropical coast of Australia. He had said Australia, and he had meant Australia!

"It's King Neptune, come up out of the bloody sea!" exclaimed one astonished Aussie as Willis walked down the main street of the town from the little harbor. And he looked it—brown, gnarled and weather-beaten—but

120

For the second time he didn't make it, but this failure didn't dim his great spirit. Here his wife greets him after he was flown to Boston and finally to New York. He had completed two thirds of the voyage when he ran out of food. (WIDE WORLD PHOTO)

he had done what he had said he would do. For the third time, he had overcome tremendous odds against his survival.

And so, at seventy-one years of age, did he retire from such strenuous activity? Not William Willis!

In 1966 he acquired an eleven-and-a-half-foot boat, little more than a rowboat, and word spread that he was at least semi-retiring from ocean-fighting. Surely that had to be true, for such a tiny boat was good for little more than cruising a local lake or river. It seemed a good thing that the adventurous old man was finally going to spend his waning years sailing about peacefully in the boat which he had christened *Little One*. No man likes to see his personal heroes die, and Willis was looked upon in that way by many men. It seemed advantageous to Willis' wife, also, who was tired of having her husband sailing off into the lonely ocean.

But it did not seem to be a tolerable course for William Willis. He hadn't bought the little boat to retire with. No, he planned to sail her across the Atlantic Ocean!

He wanted the record for having sailed the very smallest boat ever across the ocean, and in 1966 he set out on such a voyage. But the adventure ended in failure. The *Little One*'s design rendered her unstable for deep-sea sailing. Finally, the hernia which had constantly plagued Willis became agonizing, and reduced him to helplessness. The proud old man was forced to call for help. He was removed from his boat and flown back home for an emergency operation.

It was an inglorious end to a glorious life of adventure. Or was it?

Willis recovered from his operation and instituted new plans. He hired yacht builders to redesign *Little One*'s keel to make her more stable. Lead weights were added and the rigging was converted from ketch to sloop. A supporting steel truss was made to prevent a recurrence of the hernia. What he was planning became obvious, if distressing, to his many friends.

He shopped for supplies for his small boat carefully, since space was precious. In deference to his advanced age and physical condition, he included fresh water in containers, and wholemeal flour, lemon juice, olive oil, honey, and raisins, the foods he had found most nourishing on his voyages. Steel-spring arm exercisers and a set of oars were purchased to keep himself in trim.

He then told his friends what they already expected—he would attempt to sail *Little One* across the Atlantic once again. They tried to dissuade him, but it was no use. He must have such adventure to live, he told them.

In July, 1967, he boarded his vessel at Montauk, Long Island, had it towed one mile out to sea, and then cast off the lines. Swinging the rudder about, he watched the sails fill and the towboat fall astern in the freshening breeze. He aimed the bow for Plymouth, England, three thousand miles away.

At seventy-four years of age, he was off to conquer another ocean.

But once again, the voyage was doomed to fail. On October 7, 1967, when the *Little One* was two thirds of the way across the Atlantic, Willis was again forced to accept help. He had encountered unfavorable winds most of the way, and since he was behind his schedule, his food was gone. A Polish trawler picked him up and returned him to Boston.

Crushed and defeated? Not a bit of it! He was in high spirits, his eyes twinkling and a ready laugh on his lips for his misfortune.

Seven months later, on May 1, 1968, he showed again that he could not quit and would not accept defeat. Once more on the *Little One,* he sailed from Montauk Point in a third attempt to cross the Atlantic Ocean single-handed in the smallest boat ever.

As he set out he said, "Man is most challenged when he is alone."

———————————

Editor's note: A Soviet fishing vessel on September 22, 1968, reported finding a battered and deserted sailboat in the North Atlantic four hundred miles west of Ireland. Documents, including a passport, found in the tiny cabin indicated that the 11½-foot demasted boat was William Willis's *Little One*. Presumably, the sea has won the last battle.

Salvage expert Edward Ellsberg in a portrait taken at Massawa when he was a captain.
(THE NATIONAL ARCHIVES)

Edward Ellsberg

TODAY IT is estimated that nearly three quarters of all the wealth in the history of the world lies at the bottom of the sea, waiting to be reclaimed, perhaps lost forever. The hulks of tens of thousands of ships, valuable to man in wealth and knowledge, rest waiting.

A few men have devoted their lives to reclaiming these lost ships and their cargoes, in spite of the grave danger involved. One man stands out among these few. In his day he did not have the benefit of deep submersibles or of modern diving knowledge and techniques. He used equipment which, though the best available, would today be considered antiquated and hazardous to the point of foolhardiness. In accepting risks to save men and ships, which often put his own life in jeopardy, he became the dean of all salvage divers. First his fellow officer, Swede Momsen, would rescue the men—and then he would move in to rescue the vessel and the stores.

He is Admiral Edward Ellsberg, a pioneer and one of the most skillful and knowledgeable of all the hard-hat divers. A skillful writer as well, his books today still provide thrills to readers as he describes his adventures under the sea.

Already a salvage expert of world renown, stocky, hard-jawed, Lieutenant Commander Ellsberg reported for duty during World War II at the Italian port of Massawa on the Red Sea. The retreating Italians, ordered to leave nothing usable or intact for the Allied forces, had scuttled drydocks and ships, destroyed shore installations, and bombed and burned everything. The

125

port was a disaster area, a shambles. The task of opening it to shipping seemed impossible without unlimited time and labor.

Yet the job was critically important, and had to be accomplished without delay, since Italian frogmen, riding underwater bombs, had effectively closed the port of Alexandria as well. They had planted explosives on the bottoms of nearly every British ship in the port—devices which would arm and trigger themselves by the motion of the ships in the water. Nothing could move in Alexandria Harbor without the risk of blowing apart.

So the opening of Massawa was absolutely necessary. Edward Ellsberg tackled the "impossible" job. He did it with no salvage help, little equipment, and a group of civilians that included only five divers, four of whom had been hired away from motion picture stunt work.

The shore installations were brought back to working capacity first, a tough job in itself, because the sabotaging Italians had been most thorough. Then work on the hulks of ships began, the prime project being the restoration of the gigantic floating drydock now resting in fifty feet of water, a mission of critical importance, for Allied shipping in the Mediterranean needed it as a repair facility.

Shaped like a huge "U," the floating dock had a bottom one hundred feet across, six hundred feet long and fifteen feet deep. Its walls were fifteen feet thick and thirty-five feet high. Of its eight watertight sections, seven had been bombed and split open; the eighth still contained an unexploded bomb. In operation, this dock is positioned under a ship, the dock being partially submerged, then water from its compartments is pumped out, and the ship is lifted high and dry for bottom repairs.

Ellsberg tackled one of the most difficult salvage jobs of his entire career, and did it in typical Ellsberg fashion by first diving and carefully removing the bomb in the eighth chamber. Then he and his divers sealed the exploded sections and pumped air into the tanks. Slowly the giant dock lumbered to the surface as it became buoyant. In only nine days from the time he had removed the bomb, Ellsberg pronounced the drydock ready for use by the Allies. A dock which had been "permanently" destroyed by the Italians!

Edward Ellsberg's entire life was one of stubborn persistence, of never admitting that any job could not be done. At first he wanted to become a mining engineer, but his father, from whom young Edward had inherited his stubborn streak, had already chosen law as a career for his son. If the son was of firm mind, the father was even firmer.

So Edward was in his first year of pre-law at the University of Colorado

126

Edward Ellsberg standing on one of the many scuttled Italian ships during his greatest salvage effort at Massawa. (THE NATIONAL ARCHIVES)

Ellsberg is awarded the Legion of Merit by Rear Admiral James M. Irish for his work in restoring the port of Massawa for Allied shipping. (THE NATIONAL ARCHIVES)

when the major break in his life came. He won an appointment to the United States Naval Academy at Annapolis, reported there and started his studies, never suspecting the fascinating life it would lead to nor, perhaps, that it would make his name famous as an author.

On a hill overlooking the beautiful Naval Academy is a stone cross placed in memory of Commander G. W. DeLong's ill-fated expedition to the North Pole aboard the *Jeannette* in 1879. The site provided particular inspiration to Midshipman Ellsberg, as did the grave of John Paul Jones, also nearby. The significance of these areas was reflected years later in Ellsberg's fascinating books, *Hell on Ice: The Saga of the Jeannette,* and *Captain Paul.* In all, he wrote fifteen exciting books on diving, salvage, naval personalities, submarines, and the difficulties man faces when challenging the oceans of the world.

Ellsberg graduated from Annapolis in 1914, as the honor man in his class, and after brief sea duty he returned for postgraduate work at both the Academy and the Massachusetts Institute of Technology. However, before his graduate work was completed, World War I began. He put his inventive skills to work, first at the New York Navy Yard and then at the Boston Navy Yard.

A tough ocean fighter, Captain (now Admiral) Edward Ellsberg gives orders from the seat of a jeep in Egypt. (THE NATIONAL ARCHIVES)

He devised an evaporator to provide fresh water from sea water, and it was widely used. He redesigned and improved the ventilation system of the S.S. *Leviathan,* and finally, after the tragic submarine disaster, the sinking of the *S-51,* invented and tested a device which is still used in salvage work today.

When Swede Momsen located the hulk of the *S-51* with the submarine *S-1,* her sister ship, salvage attempts were promptly started under the command of the Navy's best salvage man, thirty-three-year-old Commander Edward Ellsberg. In spite of stormy seas, cases of the bends, and almost unendurable cold and depth, Ellsberg's crew—and quite often Ellsberg himself—worked for months in the dark water, diving hundreds of times to recover the bodies of the victims and then the submarine itself, 132 feet down. Forty-

This is the gigantic floating dry dock which the Italians scuttled "forever," and which Ellsberg raised at the risk of his life for the Allied Forces. Ship at right is awaiting entry for obviously needed repairs. (THE NATIONAL ARCHIVES)

ton steel pontoons were maneuvered about in the stormy sea, men dropped from sheer exhaustion, and still the salvage team worked on. They paused only during the most severe part of the winter of 1925-26, when the elements and the cruel sea became too much for the divers.

During the enforced pause in operations, Ellsberg developed a device which has since become a common tool of salvage divers. Ellsberg knew there should be a method to cut quickly through heavy steel underwater. As it was, there was only the ordinary hacksaw as a tool, which was both time-consuming and exhausting.

A salvaged craft, brought up by Ellsberg, is repaired in the dock, also brought up by Ellsberg. To the right is the Tripolitania *awaiting her turn. She was also brought up by Ellsberg after having been scuttled.* (THE NATIONAL ARCHIVES)

After many experiments, he put together an underwater cutting torch. Three high-pressure hoses extended from the surface down to the torch at the salvage job. Two of the hoses carried hydrogen and oxygen, as did any standard cutting torch, but the third carried high-pressure compressed air. In operation, the compressed air actually blasts open sufficient space in the water in which the hydrogen and oxygen can burn at a heat high enough to melt steel.

When salvage operations on the *S-51* resumed, Ellsberg was the first man down on the hulk to test his torch. It worked perfectly, and through its use the project moved forward quickly. Steel chains sent down from the steel

131

pontoons above were placed under the *S-51*, and on July 5, 1926, the hull, which had been on the bottom for nearly a year, broke the surface. At last the bodies of the remaining crewmen could be buried with appropriate honors, and the submarine could be restored to service.

With this apparently crowning achievement in salvage work behind him, Ellsberg, reaching the rank of Commander, retired to enter civilian life. But not for long. In 1927, the sleek submarine *S-4* was rammed by the destroyer *Paulding* and sent to the bottom. Ellsberg volunteered at once to head the rescue operations, having learned that men were still alive in the *S-4*. But by the time the rescue work could begin in the stormy sea, it was too late. The men on the *S-4* had died as submariners were then often expected to die— by slow suffocation, as air ran out. Disheartened, Ellsberg returned to civilian life, where he eventually embarked upon a literary career.

In 1929 he wrote *On the Bottom,* a superb adventure story about divers and shipwrecks, followed by *Thirty Fathoms Deep, Pigboats* and *S-54*. Then came *Ocean Gold* and *Spanish Ingots,* exciting books about the sea and diving. He became the most important writer of undersea lore, and was often compared to Jack London for his skill with adventure stories.

In World War II, Lt. Commander Ellsberg returned to active duty with the Navy, leading to his magnificant salvage job on the port of Massawa.

Men who challenge the ocean are of a special breed, and Ellsberg is a special man among these men. Stubborn, unable to resist that which other men have called impossible, he transferred as a full captain in the Navy to General Dwight Eisenhower's staff. His duty: Chief Salvage Officer of an area which extended from Morocco to Tunisia. It was an area littered with blasted ships, burned and ruined harbors, wreckage and desolation caused by American attacks and enemy attempts to scuttle and destroy. Oran Harbor alone held the wrecks of nearly thirty ships which had to be salvaged or removed.

Ellsberg worked until he dropped. He was finally forced to take a leave of absence for rest and recuperation, and was then assigned to duty in the United States as a supervisor of warship construction. He tolerated this important desk job for only a year, and then once again requested assignment in the war zone.

This move was a fortunate one for the Allies, for Ellsberg was directly responsible for the prevention of a costly, and potentially tragic, mistake. A huge drydock to provide harbor protection had been built for the invasion of France. It was resting partially submerged (to hide it from enemy observers), waiting to be towed in with the invasion fleet. Ellsberg understood drydocks,

132

perhaps better than any other man in the fleet. Due to his intervention, the device worked flawlessly on D-Day and provided a ready harbor for ships. Had he not forced through certain changes in its construction, it surely would have plunged to the bottom and disrupted the entire invasion plan. Many invasion soldiers remember the floating harbor at Omaha Beach on that bitter but victorious day.

Rear Admiral Ellsberg retired after World War II with an illustrious career behind him, but even then he did not stop. Turning once again to writing, this master diver and salvage expert produced more books, including the exciting *No Banners, No Bugles* and *Under the Red Sea Sun,* both about hazardous underwater exploits. In 1960, *The Far Sphere* was published.

Admiral Ellsberg will be remembered both through his diving and salvage work and his fine books, for as long as men continue to fight the sea.

Dr. Robert F. Dill, in the equipment of his trade.

(U.S. NAVY ELECTRONICS LABORATORY PHOTO)

Robert F. Dill

INITIAL TESTING for the Polaris, a missile which can be fired from beneath the sea, was under way, and oceanographers were working with the missile experts. The goal of the program was a long-range, explosive rocket which could be fired from a submerged submarine and serve as a powerful deterrent to any aggressor. In operation, the missile platform could move to any part of the sea and be ready for instant action.

Taking part in the testing program was a brilliant young oceanographer who had specialized in ocean-floor research. A skilled scuba diver, he had helped to place the giant submarine net in position underwater off San Clemente Island in Southern California. The net, placed seventy feet underwater and buoyed in position horizontally, was the same type as those used to protect harbor entrances from submarines. This one was in position to catch falling missiles.

These nets are of steel-wire mesh fine enough so even a man cannot go through. In size, this net was about one hundred and twenty feet square. Working at the very center, under the net, was the young marine geologist, Dr. Robert F. Dill.

Bubbles rose through the mesh of the net from Dill's scuba regulator as he waited in position. Then, suddenly, the bubbles stopped!

Dill felt the helpless sensation of attempting to breathe, and having no air come into his lungs. For the non-diver, it is like trying to breathe with a hand pressed over your mouth and nose. It is a helpless, hopeless feeling, par-

135

Bob Dill's trade is marine geology, and here he is shown in his "office" beneath the surface. (U.S. NAVY ELECTRONICS LABORATORY PHOTO)

ticularly if you have just exhaled your last breath, and has induced panic in many less experienced divers.

Dill, with hundreds of hours underwater, calmly removed his mouth-piece and stared at it. The mouthpiece was clear, so the failure must be some-where in the equipment on his back.

Looking up, Dill quickly discounted that as a way of escape to the sur-face. Under ideal conditions, skilled frogmen with underwater cutting equip-ment would take several minutes to get through the net. At the very edge of the net was Dill's diving buddy, John Beagles, also a skilled diver and a noted inventor of many new diving devices.

Dill tried to call to Beagles, but his grunt for assistance could not be

136

heard. By then he was in a near-faint, and his body cried for air. Fighting panic, Dill swam toward Beagles under the net. Beagles noticed his companion's rush, and realized that something was amiss. Quickly he swam toward the struggling Dill, removed his own mouthpiece and jammed it into the distressed man's mouth.

The two master divers shared Beagles' mouthpiece and air as they swam out from under the net and to the surface.

Bob Dill, handsome in a rugged, sporty, outdoorsman sort of way, does not consider this 1956 experience as coming anywhere near his most exciting moment in an ocean-fighting career.

Can you guess the type of experience this might be? Bear in mind that Dill has penetrated crushing depths in the bathyscaph *Trieste,* traveled in Cousteau's underwater saucer *Denise,* plunged to 21,000 feet in the French bathyscaph *Archimede,* and has seen hitherto unknown forms of marine life in the abysses. He is, today, one of the chief scientific observers on the new Westinghouse deep-submersible *Deepstar.*

Typically, Dill, a marine geologist first, considers his most thrilling moment to be on the day he first saw a moving river of sand on the floor of the ocean. This was an astounding discovery which suddenly brought new concepts to oceanography.

"I saw the sea floor flowing like water!" he says, still with an astonished tone in his voice. "It was an undersea process we didn't know existed, this eroding-away of the ocean floor."

This is only one of the discoveries credited to Bob Dill, one of the new breed of scientific ocean fighters who penetrate the ocean with ultra-modern equipment and years of rigorous training behind them. They have new underwater inventions and new skills and far more knowledge. Unhampered by the archaic methods used by earlier underwater explorers, these new scientists plunge deeper and stay longer and *find* that which they seek. If they should suddenly turn to treasure hunting, they would probably become wealthy beyond imagination. They do not, however, for they are enthusiastically involved in their own specific fields of ichthyology, biology, and geology. Treasures that are found—and they often do find priceless relics—are turned over to a museum.

Dill does, however, have two mementos in his home which he prizes. One is a red telephone, the other is a "coxswain's table," and both are on prominent display in Dill's living room in Southern California. Both came from the same ship, a modern ship worth millions of dollars.

Bob Dill helps to repair the net used to catch the first Polaris missile fired—the net which trapped him and nearly cost him his life.
(COURTESY DR. ROBERT DILL)

Dill was assigned by a major magazine to dive to the sunken ship shortly after she went down. He and four companions made the dive, and saw the ship still in her new paint and polish, untouched by marine growth. She rested on the bottom of the cold North Atlantic, an awesome and eerie sight, seeming for all the world ready to get underway. She still rests there, for no salvage company has ever figured a way to bring her back to the surface. By now, though, the ocean has ruined her. Eventually the ocean consumes nearly everything consigned to her depths, and hides the rest.

Only Dr. Dill did bring back the red telephone and the coxswain's table, upon which the helmsman stood when the tragic turn was made which brought her smashing into another ship and sent her to the bottom. The telephone and the table are from the bridge of the ill-fated *Andrea Doria*.

Dr. Dill received his Ph.D. from Scripps Institution of Oceanography in 1964. One of his major studies today is the attempt to determine previous

138

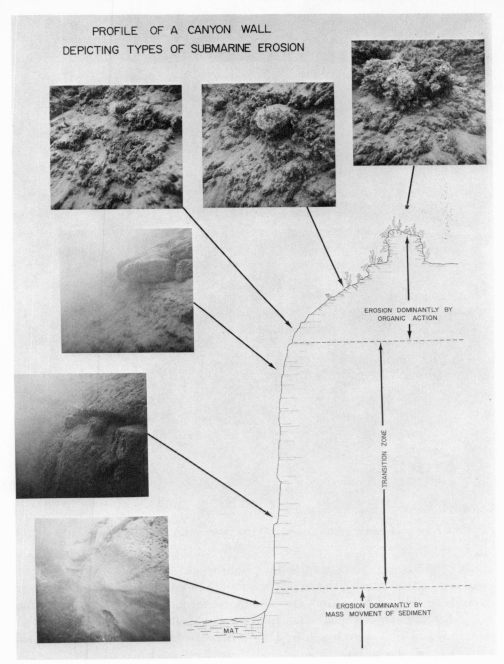

PROFILE OF A CANYON WALL
DEPICTING TYPES OF SUBMARINE EROSION

EROSION DOMINANTLY BY
ORGANIC ACTION

TRANSITION ZONE

EROSION DOMINANTLY BY
MASS MOVMENT OF SEDIMENT

MAT

A profile of a canyon wall showing different types of submarine erosion, a principal part of Dr. Dill's current research. (COURTESY DR. ROBERT DILL)

139

Dr. Dill's current research vessel Deepstar. (BOB DUNN PHOTO)

levels of the ocean. He does this by diving to old beach levels, areas which were once at the edge of the ocean, thousands or millions of years ago. From deposits he finds at these sites, he determines, through carbon-dating methods and other calculations, just when the ocean was at this level. At first, such materials and sites were found by Dill at depths of 125 feet, and dated back 13,000 years. These bits of wood and shells were evidence that the level of the ocean had risen 125 feet since then.

But, one day, exploring off Mission Bay near San Diego, Dill found slopes at seven hundred feet, obvious beaches with remnants of land and shoreline creatures. In the same murky darkness he found a cliff sixty feet high, another indication of an ancient land end. Not one to jump to conclusions, Dill searched all along the west coast of the United States, and found similar indications at the same depths. It was a new and astonishing discovery.

Still not ready to say for sure, Dill traveled to Australia, and, using deep submersible vessels such as *Deepstar,* found the very same steep clifflike formations at depths of seven hundred feet.

Dill finally concluded, and announced, that the ocean level was actually seven hundred feet lower many thousands of years ago. Vast areas of coastlines have been covered by water since then.

But how does he account for this? Where did all the extra water come from? It is Dill's opinion as a marine geologist, and an opinion now shared by others, that the water which has raised ocean levels came from glaciers melting back from their most advanced point, and from tremendous lakes which eventually dried up. Sea-life fossils indicate the previous presence of such bodies of water in the midwestern part of the United States. The same indications are found in Australia. The same is true, according to Dill, of the Sahara Desert. Dill now feels that an old surface level twelve hundred feet below the present one is possible.

It is a startling idea to imagine the United States larger and shaped differently, but that is no doubt the way things were before the ocean levels rose. It is now accepted, however, for Dill is a thorough marine geologist who never speaks until he is positive, and his colleagues know it.

In his work, as serious and often dangerous as it is, humorous situations do occur. After participating with Dr. Andreas Rechnitzer in the first sustained scientific use of the bathyscaph *Trieste,* and making several deep dives, Dr. Dill went to Puerto Rico for deep-submergence work in the French bathyscaph *Archimede.* The French pilot manned the controls while Dill served as scientific observer. The site of the dive was the Puerto Rico Trench, a 21,000-foot-deep slash off the island. Dill was particularly interested in the north wall of the trench, and its strange upsweeping currents.

To the men inside a bathyscaph, there is little difference between their sophisticated vessel and the original spheres of men like Dr. William Beebe, for their cabin is still little more than a steel ball. Modern vessels, of course, have methods of propulsion and motion up and down (Beebe's sphere was

Another view of Deepstar. (WESTINGHOUSE PHOTO)

lowered on a steel cable), and carry far more modern equipment, but it is still just a steel ball which protects the occupants. And this sphere, just like the first ones, is built with thick walls to withstand the pressures of the deep ocean.

This is one of the differences between a man in scuba gear at, let's say, two hundred feet under the surface, and a man in a steel sphere at the same depth. In scuba gear at two hundred feet—deep enough to crush a man's chest easily—the high-pressure air from the tanks fills the diver's lungs and equalizes the pressure inside his body with the pressure outside. Since the solid part of the body, excluding lung cavities, etc., is mostly water, and since water is non-compressible, the rest of the diver's body can withstand the pressure. Only the body cavities must be equalized. Sometimes they are not, and the

142

Cousteau's diving saucer Denise, *showing similarities to* Deepstar, *for Cousteau designed both vessels.* (WESTINGHOUSE PHOTO)

diver then suffers agonizing ear pains, or stomach pains, and must quickly return to the surface.

In a steel sphere, all of the ocean's pressure is expended on the walls of the sphere itself and the men inside remain, effectively, at surface pressure, since the bell is sealed at the surface.

The *Archimede*, like all bathyscaphs, was built on this principle. The *Archimede* was far below two hundred feet, well into an area of the deep ocean which would instantly smash anything unable to resist the great pressure. The trip to the bottom would take three full hours, and two hours of descent had already passed. Then it happened.

Dill felt an ice-cold drop of water hit the back of his neck. Then another and another. He recoiled.

143

The three pilots of the Deepstar, *left to right, Dick Usry, Ron Church, and Joe Thompson.*
(BOB DUNN PHOTO)

144

Realizing that if a leak were developing in the sphere, the water could streak in with a force far greater than that of a bullet and instantly kill both men long before they drowned, Dill pointed out the leak to the French pilot.

The pilot chuckled. "Condensation, Doctair," he said. "Don't worry about it at all."

The drops continued, and Dill became more concerned. If it was condensation, why were the drops so cold? The pilot was adamant—it was condensation.

Finally, by then very concerned, Dill tasted the water. It was *salty*. The pilot shrugged. It was true, he admitted, that a brand-new, untested, through-hull fitting had been installed in the sphere only the day before. Probably it was leaking slightly.

In the mind of Dr. Robert Dill there was no such thing as a *slight* leak at 21,000 feet under the ocean, but he worked under those conditions for five long hours, never sure whether the fitting was adequate. Fortunately, as the pilot had predicted, the fitting held fast. The dive was a success.

In spite of these worrisome occurrences, Dill is another of the deep-diving bathyscaph scientists who profess a complete faith in their vessels and equipment. These men do not seem afraid. Perhaps it is a native faith, or perhaps it is a necessary faith, or perhaps it is a true faith, or perhaps they are so wrapped up in their observations that they do not even think about it. But whatever the reason, the job is still quite obviously dangerous. If the sphere should rupture, or if it should snap loose from its float, or if the float should rupture, or if the vessel should become entangled with something on the bottom, or caught in a crevice, or, for that matter, entrapped by a marine creature of the depths, all would be lost. The craft is far beyond the search of any rescue effort.

Bob Dill's most current research vessel, the *Deepstar,* was built by Westinghouse Electric and is commanded by the United States Navy (Dill is a civilian scientist at the Navy Undersea Warfare Center in San Diego, California). The vessel is piloted by Ron Church, famous in his own right as an underwater photographer and diving expert. Expeditions and discoveries have been made by Dill and *Deepstar* throughout the world. He has worked in many deep-submersibles, but he calls *Deepstar* the finest one of them all. With Dr. Francis P. Shepard, Dill has written of some of his findings, and of his feelings about deep-diving scientific work, in his latest book, *Submarine Canyons and Other Sea Valleys.*

Dill is a member of the board of directors of General Oceanographics,

Two stages of the construction of Deepstar, *with bottom photo showing hull internal machining at Westinghouse.* (WESTINGHOUSE PHOTO)

Inc., a company which conducts underwater geological studies around the world, and a company he helped found. Major oil companies are, of course, interested in the work of General Oceanographics because of the potential offshore oil reserves it may discover.

Dr. Dill has personally seen (at five hundred-yard intervals) every bit of the sea floor off Southern California, from the Mexican border to Point Conception. Other work for the company has taken him to the waters of the Mississippi Delta, Venezuela, the Feather River and Monterey Bay in Northern California. A highly proficient underwater photographer, Dill has been called upon by many major publications to shoot still and motion pictures underwater. He was one of the chief contributors to the motion picture *Hunters of the Deep*, and his underwater footage has been used by several film production companies.

In his off-duty hours, Dill lectures to university groups on the science of marine geology. Although he is considered to be one of the new group of very advanced oceanographers, he still feels he is only laying the groundwork for later scientists. Young people who are not yet sure of their future careers will study all the fields open to them, and some will select oceanography. Then a few of these will turn to marine geology as their specific study; and they will come to look upon Dr. Robert Dill, though a "new-breed" man against the sea, as a pioneer.